Where is the Nightglow?
Poetry and Paintings

Paul Klinger

Grosvenor House
Publishing Limited

All rights reserved
Copyright © Paul Klinger, 2025

The right of Paul Klinger to be identified as the author of this
work has been asserted in accordance with Section 78
of the Copyright, Designs and Patents Act 1988

The book cover is copyright to Paul Klinger

This book is published by
Grosvenor House Publishing Ltd
Link House
140 The Broadway, Tolworth, Surrey, KT6 7HT.
www.grosvenorhousepublishing.co.uk

This book is sold subject to the conditions that it shall not, by way of
trade or otherwise, be lent, resold, hired out or otherwise circulated
without the author's or publisher's prior consent in any form of
binding or cover other than that in which it is published and
without a similar condition including this condition being
imposed on the subsequent purchaser.

This book is a work of fiction. Any resemblance to
people or events, past or present, is purely coincidental.

A CIP record for this book
is available from the British Library

Paperback ISBN 978-1-83615-238-5
eBook ISBN 978-1-83615-239-2

INTRODUCTION

I've named this book *Where is the Nightglow?* based on an erroneous impression, the true facts being much more prosaic than my imagination. It was during the pandemic of 2020 onwards, and when I looked out of the bedroom window of my house, southwards to West London, I was under the impression that a nighttime glow I had seen in the sky before the pandemic, had disappeared.

The truth of the matter, although I can't verify it, is that what I was seeing was not the glow of all the buildings in central and West London, but lighting used in Wembley Stadium at night to encourage the grass of the pitch to be healthy!

The poem "Where is the Nightglow?" describes my feelings about the lights of London being effectively switched off by the pandemic. Other than that, there are many poems about nature, with perhaps not as many satirical poems as in my first two poetry books, *Alone in the City* and *My Abstract Life*.

This book is arranged in alphabetical order. All of the poems herein are featured on my Instagram page, @paulklingerpoetry. Each chapter starts with a painting by myself appropriate to one of the poems in the chapter.

I have only delved into the world of Instagram since 2019, a year after my last poetry book, *My Abstract Life*, was published. In that year I spent some time in the very comfortable Wellington Hospital in London, where I had time and space to paint and write poetry.

During a visit from my friend, Ruben, he suggested I should put my art on Instagram, which I have done ever since. Then, a year or so later, I did the same with my poetry. This book serves as an archive for my Instagram poetry, whereas my Instagram art page serves as an archive for most of my paintings. There are almost 800 pictures on my Instagram art page, @klinger459, and my poetry page can be found at @paulklingerpoetry.

Since my last book was published in 2018, I have retired, so have more time to pursue other interests, one of which is learning to play the piano. I have found that music composition has been another outlet for my creativity. I have recorded many YouTube videos of my performances of these compositions, for example, a search of 'Paul Klinger The Bumble Bee' should reveal one. I have not yet mastered how to professionally produce such videos, as will be obvious when viewing them!

I would like to thank my partner, Angela, for her steadfast faith in my poetry and art, and her helpful musical guidance, coming from a talented and experienced musician.

Paul Klinger
Stanmore
2025

CONTENTS

Chapter 1: Autumn in the Woods	1
A Billion Stars	3
All the Philosophers	4
Alone in the Woods	5
An Appreciation	6
Atlas of the World	7
Autumn in the Woods	9
Avenue of Trees	11
Chapter 2: Blow, Fresh Air	13
Babbling Brook	15
Birdbath	16
Birds' Nest	17
Black Clouds	19
Blow, Fresh Air	21
Bluebell Woods	23
Book	25
Bunker in my Mind	28
Chapter 3: Castle in the Mist	31
Candle Flame	33
Castle in the Mist	35
Charge Me!	37
Clouds Behind the Chimneys	38
Come Out!	40
Come, Enter all Smiles	41
Country House	43

Crepuscular Rays	45
Crescent Moon	47
Croci on my Lawn	48
Crocus and the Lake	50
Crow	51
Cruise Control	53

Chapter 4: Dappled Light in the Woods — 55

Dandelion Seeds	57
Dappled Light in the Woods	59
Dark Clouds and Rain	61
Dark Nights	62
Diary	64
Dictionary	66
Distant View	68
Do I Belong in the City	69
Do the Birds Know?	71
Documenting You	72
Don't Blame the Rain	73
Don't Bombard Me	75
Drama in the Trees	77

Chapter 5: Elysian Fields — 79

Elysian Fields	81

Chapter 6: Fallen Tree — 83

Fallen Tree	85
Finding you in the city	87
Flower in the Forest	89
Fluffy White Clouds	90
Flying High	91
Forget the Bad Days	92
From my Kitchen Window	93

Chapter 7: Gilded Mirror — 95

- Gap in the Hedge — 97
- Gilded Mirror — 99
- Girl in the Painting — 101

Chapter 8: Heron — 103

- Haunting Music — 105
- Heron — 106
- Hoping Things Get Better — 108
- House for Sale — 109
- How will we be Remembered? — 111

Chapter 9: I Feed the Birds — 113

- I Feed the Birds — 115
- I Switch on the Light — 117
- If all the Minds in the World — 119
- If I Seem Distant — 121
- Imagination — 122
- In Defence of the Realm — 124
- In the Garden — 125
- Is there a God to whom you pray? — 127

Chapter 10: Just Another Day — 129

- Job Satisfaction — 131
- Just Another Day — 133

Chapter 11: London by Night — 135

- Lamppost Number Twenty-two — 137
- London By Night — 139
- Lonely Path — 141
- Look Up at the Sky — 143
- Lost on the Mountain — 145

Chapter 12: Magic Horse — 147

- Magic Horse — 149
- Magician — 151
- Major Route — 153
- Message in a Bottle — 155
- Missing the Sea — 157
- Misty Lake — 158
- Moon — 160
- Mother's Love — 162
- My Abstract Painting — 163
- My Education — 164
- My Friend, the Little Bird — 166
- My Ornaments — 168
- My Purpose in the World — 170
- My Yucca Plant — 171
- Mystical Music — 172

Chapter 13: Nymph of the Winds — 175

- Night Sky — 177
- Nymph of the Winds — 178

Chapter 14: Out of the Houses — 181

- Oak Tree — 183
- One Day we Shine — 185
- One o'clock, Struck the Bell — 187
- Out of the Houses — 189
- Over My Fence and Far Away — 191

Chapter 15: Poor little Buttercup — 193

- Pandemic Walk — 195
- Parakeet — 197
- Pollarded Tree — 198

Poor Little Buttercup	200
Pounding Pavements	201
Procession	203
Puff of Wind	205

Chapter 16: Regent's Park — 207

Regent's Park	209
Rattler	211
Reasons to be Cheerful	212
Red Kite	213
Rhythmic	215

Chapter 17: Silk Stream — 217

She-Buddha	219
Silk Stream	220
Sitting by the Lake	222
Sitting in the Garden	224
Sparkles	226
Spider's Web	227
Spirits	229
Strange Times	231

Chapter 18: Twinkling Star — 233

Take off your Headphones	235
The Ferryman	236
Tower	238
Twinkling Star	240
The Umbrella	242

Chapter 19: Where is the Nightglow? — 243

Walk	245
Walk Through Nature	246

Waterfall	248
Waves on the Shore	249
Weeping Willow	251
What Happened to the Birds?	252
What Happened to Your Dreams?	254
What Three Words?	256
When I can't Sleep	257
When I hear Birdsong	259
When Normal Life Resumes	261
Where is the Night Glow?	263
Chapter 20: You are my Destination	**265**
You are my Destination	267

Chapter 1
Autumn in the Woods

A Billion Stars

A billion are the stars in the sky,
A million are the grass blades;
There are thousands of cities in the world
But only one of you were made.

A billion are the lights in the sky,
A million are the blades of green,
There are thousands of places all lit up
But your eyes are the brightest I've seen.

A billion are the words that have been written;
A million are the books to read;
There are a thousand volumes of reference,
But you are all I need.

A billion are the thoughts I have thought,
A million are the words I could write;
There are a thousand expressions of love,
And I'm going to start tonight.

All the Philosophers

All the philosophers, and therapists,
And psychiatrists in the land;
All the professors and doctors
Don't understand,

All the physicists and chemists,
And geologists that they send;
All the engineers and technicians,
Can't comprehend,

All the accountants, and actuaries,
And mathematicians who are about;
All the statisticians and economists,
Can't work it out,

All the journalists and editors,
All the authors and writers;
All the novelists and publishers,
Can't decipher,

All the experts in the world,
Even for an expensive fee,
Can never work out the connection
There is between you and me.

Alone in the Woods

Alone in the Woods
Amongst trees, so old.
I want to hear their stories,
If only they could be told.

There is spirituality present;
The birds know it well,
And so too do the animals
As far as I can tell.

I met a fox;
Our eyes briefly met.
His gaze told me
That I'm not ready yet

To learn about God's ways,
Ways he already knew.
Ways that are known,
By the very very few.

But the trees know
And so do the birds,
And that's why they make
The most beautiful sound heard.

An Appreciation

Sometimes I can't use paintings
To illustrate a scene.
So words have to be used
To describe what I've seen.

The setting sun
On the distant trees,
The fluffy white clouds
Nudged on by the breeze.

A slight disturbance of the leaves,
In the moving air
Makes me want to leave my room
And be just there!

Trees of different colours
And shapes and sizes;
I watch a distant plane
As it slowly rises

Into the vast sky
Changing colour in the sunset.
I want to grab every last bit
Of daylight I can get.

And when the sun goes down
And the blue sky turns to grey,
I remember everything I've seen
And pray for the new day.

Atlas of the World

I could travel to distant lands
Where the sun shines down on golden sands.
Or see snow atop mountains high
Where eagles soar and condors fly.

I could visit far-off places
With vast vistas and open spaces,
Where the crops grow in wide-open prairies,
Or see dappled woods which entertain the fairies.

I could search for glaciers of ice
In lands so cold which still entice;
Or cross lakes fifty miles long
Where herons and waterfowl belong.

I could arrive to see the dawn
In stately homes with manicured lawns.
Or see haunted castles, well-fortified
And hear the sounds of maidens' sighs.

I could journey to beautiful palaces
And see knights of old with swords and chalices,
With wonderful paintings on the wall
Of the great and good, pictures all.

I could cross deserts so dry
And find an oasis where camels lie,
Seeing ancient monuments of rock and stone
And hear the sound of the wind as it moans.

I could visit oriental climes
Seeing magic carpets with cords entwined,
Watching glittering lanterns on magic boats,
Hearing tinkling bells as they float.

Let's face it the world is immense,
And can be visited at great expense,
But it's easier to sit with my cat, curled,
Looking at my atlas of the world.

Autumn in the Woods

Autumn is here, some say fall,
And I'm overwhelmed by it all.
By the magic carpet on the ground;
Yellows and reds all around.

Also, some browns and green,
Branches bare where leaves have been,
And when the sun comes out as well
There's beauty, more than I can tell.

Acorns drop from the mighty oaks,
And hug the ground like strange cloaks.
Conkers also are on the ground
Painted in colours of reddish-brown.

I have fantasies I can confide,
Of taking a magic carpet ride
On the golden rug of leaves,
Through the woods I'd weave.

All the woodland creatures smile
And take time out for a while,
From their woodland tasks
To watch as I fly past.

The carpet lowers me down,
And I go home with a frown,
Because I'm leaving my friends
I didn't want it to end.

But, fear not, when the season changes
And for three months winter rages,
Beauty, again, will show
In the pure, white, soft snow.

Avenue of Trees

I walk through the avenue of trees;
I do not know their names.
My arboreal knowledge is incomplete,
For that I take the blame.

I asked what they've done
Since I saw them last.
I know their present;
I want to know their past.

They told me of the hours
From sunrise to sunset.
They told me of every bird,
Who on their branches they'd met

They told me of the stories
The birds had to tell.
They told me about squirrels
And snails in their shell.

There was too much to write down
In any chronicle or book,
So what I remembered
Was all that I took

From that arboreal encounter
Through that arcadian place,
And because I was thinking
It slowed up my pace,

So that people passed me by,
And wondered about the delay.
He's not as young as he was
Is what they'd probably say.

But what was in my head
Was better than their speed.
Maybe my muscles weren't exercised
But it's my imagination I feed.

Because if they slowed down
And didn't speak to their fellow,
So they could concentrate
On colours red, green and yellow

They'd understand maybe more
About nature abounding,
And listen to life around them,
And how wonderful it's sounding.

Chapter 2
Blow, Fresh Air

Babbling Brook

The babbling of the brook,
The whisper of the breeze,
The patter of the raindrops,
Puts me at my ease.

The howling of the wind,
The crash of the thunder,
The clatter of the hail,
Nature casts asunder.

The buzzing of the bees,
The tweeting of the birds,
The rustling of the leaves,
Nicest sound I've heard.

The wash of the waves,
The cry of the gulls,
The crunching of the pebbles,
My tension is annulled.

The hoot of the owl,
The squeak of the bats,
The silence of the night,
Daylight – please come back!

Birdbath

There's a birdbath in my garden,
It was me who put it there.
It's the sort of birdbath
You can buy anywhere.

I like to watch the birds wash,
I watch the way they behave.
They do the same things as me
Except they don't shave.

They perch on the rim,
And look down at the water.
They never seem so sure,
But then they think, *I ought to*.

So they have a little splash
And they have a little drink,
And as I'm watching them,
I have a little think.

I think , I hope they're happy,
I hope they're grateful to me,
For providing washing facilities,
And, after all, they're free!

Birds' Nest

Home sweet home,
Was the birds' nest,
But why was it deserted?
Some tragedy, I guessed.

Four white eggs,
Nestled there, not hatched.
Lying on warm feathers,
Lovingly attached.

An engineered miracle
By our feathered friends.
Grass, woven together;
But the idyll had to end.

***

Here we are,
In our constructions,
Safe as houses,
Safe from abductions.

No predators can penetrate
Solid brick walls,
But beware, are we protected
Within these halls?

Beware of what life brings
Into our delicate minds.
Therein lies the danger,
I think you'll find.

Black Clouds

There are black clouds above you
But look, there are blue skies ahead
Don't let the present suppress you
Look to the future instead.

Like the flowers, which close their petals
When the sun goes away
They don't give up –
They wait for the new day.

Like the birds, who go to sleep
When the black night comes in,
Dreaming of the dawn
When everything will begin.

Like the hedgehog, who doesn't die
When winter draws near.
He hibernates and sleeps,
Without any fear.

Like the birds, which migrate
During the winter freeze,
But they'll be back
And will be at their ease.

Look, here comes the sun
And the sky's turning blue.
Nature is renewing
And so should you.

Blow, Fresh Air

Blow, fresh air!
Bring me the scent of roses
Bring me honeysuckle fragrance
And I'll have no care

Fresh air, fresh air
Blowing from the north
I feel the breeze
Bring it forth.

Blow, fresh air!
Bring me the scent of jasmine
Bring me lavender fragrance
Life seems so fair.

Fresh air, fresh air
Blowing from the south
I feel it on my face
I drink it with my mouth.

Blow, fresh air!
Bring me the scent of cut grass
Bring me mint fragrance
Joy everywhere.

Fresh air, fresh air
Blowing from the east
I feel it satisfies my hunger
Just like a feast.

Blow, fresh air!
Bring me the scent of chamomile
Bring me lemon fragrance
For me to share.

Fresh air, Fresh air
Blowing from the west
I feel the sensation
It is just the best.

Bluebell Woods

What will be?
What shall we see?
How long will we walk
Talking our clever talk?

We know not what's ahead
Or when our book will be read
What is our destiny
Is not up to you or me.

But one thing I know
Is wherever we go
Up ahead is a wood
Filled with things so good

Filled with bluebells
And I can tell
That there'll be a new dawn
Stretching out like a lawn

Feast our eyes on sunlight
No more dark, just bright
Fragrance from flowers
Giving us new powers

So do not worry
Don't dawdle or hurry
It's waiting up ahead
Let yourself be led

To this paradise
It's no sacrifice
Everyone will be there
So don't ever fear.

Book

It started as a letter
Not really an idea;
But then I had inspiration,
And made a syllable appear.

The syllable seemed lonely,
And wanted some friends.
I put two together,
And another at the end.

I realised this was a word
It had meaning and sound,
And I knew then, that
On a journey I was bound.

What if I combined words,
Two or three or more?
And finished with a comma;
It needed a name for sure.

How about "phrase"?
Yes, that will do;
But what it could do itself,
I didn't have a clue.

So I thought and I thought,
Several phrases, followed by a dot;
Which I'd call a full stop,
I thought, I'll give this a shot.

What should I call it?
It took me a while,
Then the word "sentence"
Made me smile.

And all these sentences,
One after the other,
Might make sense,
Until you had a shudder,

And could say no more.
T'was a group, needing a name,
Forming a group of thoughts,
Which were all the same.

"Paragraph", of course,
What else could it be?
But I had to keep on
Maybe to eternity.

But no, I could stop
Sometime before then.
I could have many paragraphs,
Two, three, ten.

But eventually, I knew
I would have to pause;
And collect my thoughts,
Like a sea reaching its shores.

And that's when I knew
What I would call this collection
Of sentences, paragraphs
Maybe a section?

But no, I came across
A grander-sounding name.
It would be a chapter,
The end of the game.

I'd put all the chapters together,
And call it a book.
How clever I was;
What an effort it took.

But alas, somebody
Quietly pointed out
It had been done before,
There were plenty about.

So that's a shame; I thought
I'd invented something new.
Oh well, I'll have to think
Of something else to do.

Bunker in my Mind

I have a concrete bunker
In my head
It's not real concrete,
It's imaginary, instead.

But its purpose is the same
It keeps everyone out.
I really don't care
If they scream and shout.

In this bunker
Is poetry, and art,
And my imagination
Straight from the heart.

I went there
Just the other day
When I was bored
With things they say.

In my bunker are all nice things
It's where I go when I can't sleep.
I keep on adding to it
It goes down quite deep.

If somebody says something nice
Into my bunker it goes.
It's got things that please me
That nobody knows.

When things are bad
I go in and bolt the door.
Which is very strong
Going from ceiling to floor.

To the outside world
A glazed look in my eyes,
Means I'm in my bunker
That's what it signifies.

Who needs pills
With a bunker like mine?
Just a visit down there
And I'll be fine.

It doesn't require travel
So it's perfect for now,
You can try it too,
If I show you how

Chapter 3
Castle in the Mist

Candle Flame

When the candle flame flickers
Atop tall candles of wax,
There are shadows on the ceiling,
And spirituality is at a max.

When the candle flame flickers
Sabbath is brought into the home,
Whether it's a humble dwelling,
or a mansion with a dome.

When the candle flame flickers
Scriptures are read,
And the children are imbued,
With stories in their heads.

When the candle flame flickers
No work is done,
And the family are united,
As if they are one.

When the candle flame flickers
It can be seen from the street;
So tell the people
whoever it is you meet.

When the candle flame flickers
Nobody shall do harm,
Nobody shall be stressed,
Everybody will be calm.

When the candle flame flickers
Children gather round the table,
Learning about tales of old
and well-known fables.

When the candle flame flickers
And the day draws to an end,
All troubles are forgotten,
And our minds are on the mend.

Castle in the Mist

I look into the distance
As I sit upon a hill,
I spot a castle surrounded by mist,
I must go there, I will.

I'm sure that in that castle
All my dreams will come true.
It's what I've always wanted,
And I need a vista that's new.

I walk for many hours,
It gets closer as I advance.
The mist begins to clear;
I feel as if in a trance.

Imagining coats of arms,
I will feel as grand as a lord.
I shall invite all to banquets,
Which I'll be able to afford.

But as I got closer,
The mist began to clear,
And I saw there was no castle
A block of flats was there.

Containing hundreds of people,
Not just my entourage;
My illusions were shattered
And they were so very large.

But I'll tell the people inside
Whatever troubles you bear,
From that distant hill
One thing is very clear.

You live in a place of magic,
To live here was my dream.
Where you live is a palace,
Fit for a king and queen.

Always remember that,
When life gets you down.
From the top of that hill
You're the luckiest people around.

Charge Me!

I need to find my charger
When I've had a bad day.
I'll plug myself into my charger
To make the bad things go away

Trickle-charge is no good,
I need the full blast.
My spirits need a super-boost,
And they need it very fast.

My charger's got several names
Sometimes it's called red wine.
Just put the charger in front of me
And plug it into the line.

It only takes ten minutes
Then I'm full steam ahead.
The trouble is, next morning
I'll get it in the head.

Clouds Behind the Chimneys

The clouds pile up
Behind the chimney stacks,
On the roofs of the houses,
Side-to-side, back-to-back.

Strange shapes, daunting,
Moving at their own pace,
The sun behind them
Watching the race.

A murmuration of starlings
Somewhere up there,
I don't know if they can see me
I don't know if they care.

A pigeon sits
On a house's aerial,
Watching all that happens
Quite ethereal.

A rainbow appears,
Water droplets in the spectrum.
People don't notice,
I wonder if I should tell them.

Parakeets squawk by,
Missing their natural climes,
Talking to each other
about better times.

The rain comes again
A brief sharp shower.
The birds don't care,
But the people cower.

All nature is out today
You can see her all around,
And nothing else matters,
When the elements abound.

Come Out!

All those in houses
All those in the flats
Singles, partners, spouses
Come out!

All those in schools
All those in colleges
Heed the calls
Come out!

Come enjoy the air
Come enjoy the sun
Feel the gentle breeze
Enjoy, everyone!

All those in hospitals
All those in clinics
Let's hear the footfall
Come out!

All those in factories
All those in offices
Have a break, it's satisfactory
Come out!

Come enjoy the blue sky
Come enjoy the flowers
Feast your eyes on colours
Feel your renewed power

Come, Enter all Smiles

Enter into the gates,
The Tudor arch so high;
Come in, all smiles,
You will leave with a sigh.

Breathe in the fragrance
From the flowers, so plentiful;
All the colours of the rainbow,
So very beautiful.

Feast at the table,
Succulent food, fine wine,
Made from the grapes
Of the very best vines.

The warm sultry night,
Bright stars in the sky,
A waxing moon,
Your spirits are high.

Joke with the hosts,
Tell tales of yesteryear;
Listen to music
So beautiful to hear.

Dance under the moon
Between statues, around trees,
Forget your troubles,
Be totally at ease.

Beautiful faces,
Of all different ages
Dressed with elegance,
From the fashion pages.

Everyone is your friend,
Nobody wishes you harm,
Whoever speaks to you
Does so with charm.

You'll remember this time
An experience not to forget,
So make sure you store up
Memories to collect.

Say your farewells,
Au revoir, not goodbye,
You came, all smiles
You'll leave with a sigh.

Inspired by an engraving on a Tudor arch near my home:
"Come, enter all smiles, depart, only sighs".

Country House

The house nestles in the country,
Surrounded by fields and a wood.
The sun shines through the windows
Leaving me feeling so very good.

The views go on for miles;
In the distance is a church spire.
During the day my spirits
Get lifted higher and higher.

But at night the house changes,
And creatures suddenly appear
From the woods and the fields
If you listen you can hear

Their strange murmurs and cries,
And a tapping on the glass.
Is it a branch blowing in the wind,
Or a spirit from my past?

There's a moaning outside,
Is it an animal caught in a trap?
The rain pours down in buckets
I hear a thunderclap.

I cannot sleep till dawn
When there is a beautiful sunrise;
The golden rays shining through
as the birdsong multiplies.

There are bluebells and snowdrops
And the buzz of honeybees.
There is a warm gentle breeze
Rustling the leaves in the trees.

Until night falls again,
The moon covered by dark clouds.
There is no light at all outside,
I swear I can see shrouds.

Are there ghosts between the trees,
Or is it something I'm imagining?
The breeze turns into a gale,
And sets everything rattling.

They're coming to get me,
I'm not sure I can survive.
I'll be very very lucky
if I get out of this place alive.

So the next day I pack my things
I'm heading back to town,
Where I can look out of my window,
And see people walking up and down.

Instead of country I'll have my garden.
I can plant oaks, cypress and willow.
At night there will be streetlights and
I'll sleep soundly on my pillow.

Crepuscular Rays

Crepuscular rays
Shining onto the ground;
If I travelled there
Would a pot of gold be found?

If I sail there
Across the sea,
This is what I would hope
Would be waiting for me:

A lost love
A forgotten thought
A remembered sensation
A word that I caught.

An evocative fragrance
A subtle taste
A beautiful view
A meal I couldn't waste.

A missed companion
A long-lost friend
A passed loved one
A message I didn't send.

Crepuscular rays
Please shine on me.
Show me, when I get there
What I want to see.

A discarded gift
A forgotten book
A quote from a scholar
A loving look.

An unvisited land
A forgotten pleasure
A tasted drink
A song that I treasured.

A relaxing place
A happy time
A poem I created
A picture that was fine,

If I sail there
Across the sea
That is what I hope
Would be waiting for me.

You can go there
Don't expect pots of gold;
Far more valuable
Are the things just told.

Crescent Moon

The crescent moon and the evening star
Guide me home from distances far.
The early star is the first in the night,
Followed by myriads of twinkling lights.

When I sleep they shine on me,
Whilst in my dreams I wander free;
Reconstructing events of my day,
In some weird and wonderful way.

The next day I work on my plan,
Trying to do the best I can.
The moon and the stars wait,
And when night falls don't hesitate;

In the night before I sleep,
I creep across to have a peep
At my friends shining in the sky;
Then, happily, down I lie.

Croci on my Lawn

Lovely little croci,
Growing on my lawn,
Your lives are too short,
But I don't intend to mourn.

Instead I'll tell you
About what happens as you sleep,
About flowers that came after you,
So joyful, that I don't weep.

The snowdrops came,
So soon after the snow,
Pure white, so brilliant,
I didn't want them to go.

Then came the daffodils,
Nodding in the breeze,
Bright yellow, radiant
They put me at my ease.

Next, lovely bluebells,
In my garden and the woods,
Getting lost amongst their stems,
Is what I'd like, if I could.

But I know that while you sleep,
God comes to you,
During the long summer,
To tell you what to do.

He tells you how
To brighten up my day
And soothe my mind,
Making troubles go away,

Next time you show your faces
Orange, purple and white,
Which give me so much pleasure
After a long restless night.

So when you come again,
God willing, next spring,
There'll be even more delight
In the joy that you bring.

Crocus and the Lake

The wind blows strongly
And the winter flowers are afraid.
The crocus shuts its little face
Frightened of the noise that's made.

But I go to see the lake;
On its surface are water sprites,
To them the wind is a joy
As they dance with all their might.

Some people just see moving water,
But mystical people see fairies,
Performing ballet on the water,
Dancing until they are weary.

We don't just see water,
It's not just nothing at all.
We can see nature's magic
And it holds us in its thrall.

So when the crocus cries,
Because of the nasty breeze,
I tell it, "Wait for the sunshine
Then you'll be at your ease."

Crow

Come, my friend, have your fill.
Take food for your family.
Let me share what I have
So you leave me happily.

I'll leave it under the oak tree;
It's only an apple core,
And if it's not enough for you
I'll be back tomorrow with more.

I'm only here when the sun shines,
And that's when my friend will know
That I'll be there to help.
After all, he's only a crow.

But the crow and I are friends.
He knows I have a favourite spot.
He knows what food I'll bring,
Even though it's not a lot.

But it's enough to fill him,
And his wife and children too.
I stood there watching him grab it,
And then, away he flew.

We never exchange words,
But we have an understanding.
He knows I'm watching him
When he takes off and when he's landing.

He doesn't speak English,
And I don't speak crow,
But a common language
Between us seems to flow.

I go back to my work,
With a warm feeling inside,
Knowing the crow will think of me
As he flies far and wide.

Cruise Control

My life is on cruise control,
But I need to switch to manual;
I need to override bad thoughts
And good days to be automatic.

The world's on cruise control,
But it needs to switch to manual.
We need to override global warming,
And conservation to be automatic.

Politics is on cruise control,
But it needs to switch to manual.
We need to override wars,
And peace to be automatic.

Our relationship is on cruise control,
But we need to switch to manual.
We need to override complacency,
'I love you' should be automatic.

Chapter 4
Dappled Light in the Woods

Dandelion Seeds

I blew on the dandelion
And the seeds flew up and away;
Where they eventually land
Nobody can say.

One seed flew far away,
Buffeted by the breeze.
It landed in a garden
And settled down with ease.

But a robin said to the seed,
"Do not take root here,
Go away from this place,
Because the owners are in despair".

So the seed took off again
But the next place it came down,
A pigeon told of misery
In all houses in the town.

It tried another garden,
But a magpie said, "Move again!
Don't stay with these people,
Who are in so much pain."

In the next place it went
A wren said, "You've got it right!
The people in this house
Have happiness and light."

But the seed said to the bird,
"This is not the place for me.
I will fly back to that house
That is full of misery."

"Because that house needs me,
When my petals become bright
To them I will bring joy
And I will make everything right."

Dappled Light in the Woods

Dappled light in the woods,
Shining in patches on the ground.
Should I walk through the beams
Or make my way around?

There's movement in the sunbeam,
It's a dancing dragonfly.
Or is it a wood sprite, or elf,
Who can be rather shy?

He's an accomplished dancer,
He does it when I'm not there,
But he always has an audience
The foxes or the deer.

The dappled light is his stage,
The sunbeam his limelight,
His audience is the animals,
And he always does it right.

Dancing in the sunshine,
Or in the light of the moon,
His music is the wind,
Playing her special tune.

And when the show is over,
And the animals go to bed,
He just cannot stop
So he sings to himself instead.

I love the little dragonfly,
Or is it the wood sprite?
Come, try to spot him,
In the early morning light.

Dark Clouds and Rain

Dark clouds and rain,
Will the light come again?
But what's that up above
A chink of light that I love.

Dense nettles and weeds,
Will I ever see the colour I need?
But what's that over there?
A pretty flower, so dear.

A dense book sends me to sleep,
Will there ever be any words I can keep?
But what's that in chapter seven
Some words sent from heaven.

Tuneless music, a drone,
I'm listening to when alone.
But what's that, a melody
So beautiful, it raises me.

Unfriendly people ignoring me,
Nothing hopeful I can see.
But what's that, a friendly word
The best thing I've heard.

Bad times, it seems no hope,
Difficult for people to cope.
But what's that not far away
Coming around soon – a magic day.

Dark Nights

The days are shorter
The nights are long
Life seems harder
But I could be wrong.

My lights are brighter
Shutting out the gloom
Some white, some colour
Filling the room.

My music is louder
I compose a song
The tempo is faster
Crescendos are long.

Imagination is stronger
In many different ways
To make my mind wonder
Along coves and bays.

Outside it's darker
But my mind is bright
It's not starker
Because I see the light.

It'll soon be winter
And it'll be cold
And there's danger
So I'm told.

We're all getting older
Some say more wise
Is it better
Or is it all lies?

I replenish the feeder
So the birds will come
They are so much needier
Each and every one.

The cats are bolder
They watch my friends
Who may be feathered
But that's where it ends.

My garden is busier
With cats and birds
But the road is quieter
Can't be heard.

And it's darker
Others don't use lights
But I'm livelier
Throughout the night.

Diary

When someone says a nice thing
When the music's good and bells ring
When the sun shines and you want to sing
Write it in a diary.

When the flowers are bright
When you see a good sight
When everything seems right
Write it in a diary.

When all you get is insults
When you just can't get a result
When everything you do is at fault
Read good things in your diary.

When life doesn't seem worthwhile
When things seem pointless and futile
When you just can't force a smile
Read good things in your diary.

When everybody's on your side
When you want to be seen, not hide
When you're dynamic, occupied
Write it in a diary.

When the air is fresh and your walk is brisk
When it really is worth taking a risk
When you're in love and receive a kiss
Write it in a diary.

When you're the subject of a complaint
When you feel unwell and want to faint
When you feel so tired but people won't wait
Read the good things in your diary.

When the news you read is really bad
When everything makes you feel so sad
When you feel insane and going mad
Read the good things in your diary.

When things are good, write them down,
There'll be times when you wear a frown,
But good times will soon come around,
Because it says so in your diary.

Dictionary

On my bookshelf
There is a dictionary.
I looked inside
To learn about me.

I found a word
Which described my mind,
So I decided to continue
To see what I could find.

I found a word
To describe my heart.
It helped me understand
My feelings when we part.

I found a word
To describe my mood.
The lows, highs,
Important to include.

I found a word
To describe my love
Of the sun, the sea
And the skies above.

I found a word
To describe my soul
It helped me know
That it was whole.

I'm going to use my dictionary
To describe everything,
Whatever life throws at me,
Whatever it brings.

Distant View

Look into the distance,
Can you see your dream?
You can see it in the sunshine;
Bright lights make it gleam.

Do you think you should go
Down that path so difficult and long?
When you eventually arrive,
Will it all go terribly wrong?

Maybe it's better to stay
Safe inside the open door.
If you arrived at your destination,
You can't dream any more.

Do I Belong in the City

Pavements instead of grass
Puddles instead of ponds
Is this city
Where I belong?

Lampposts not trees
People, not birds
Traffic, not birdsong
Different sounds are heard.

People rushing about
Business to be done
Wildlife is the same
Each and every one.

Streets in the city
Lead to another road
A path through the woods
Leads to a witch's abode.

Buildings in the city
Made of stone and brick
In the woods are hideouts
Made of branches so thick.

City traffic lights
Going red, amber, green
In nature, flowers' colours
Are a sight to be seen.

City people get angry
With what you do or say
In the woods, creatures
Will get out of your way.

City folk are human
Except dogs and cats
Go into the forest
To get away from that.

Look up in the city
You may possibly see sky
No obstructions in the woods
So birds can really fly.

When all is built up
And you really need some air
Just go into nature
Calm will be there.

Do the Birds Know?

Two pigeons sitting on the roof
Lovebirds, they are not aloof.
They cuddle up, close together
At all times, whatever the weather.

There is the robin, let him sing.
He knows nothing of social distancing.
Does he know, does he suspect
That his human friends are so upset?

To him the world has not changed,
Nothing in nature has rearranged.
Does he notice that we walk apart?
Still he sings with all his heart.

And the blue tit, and the wren,
They still visit my garden, even when
My world has changed, but not theirs,
For them there are no fears.

Blackbirds, robin and magpie,
Let me watch you all fly
Do not worry about the rest,
It's spring, so build your nest.

Make sure your babies survive
Then through the summer they can thrive,
And when grown, come visit me;
All this will be over, you'll see.

Documenting You

A flyer is too short
To describe your effect on me;
A brochure is too brief
To explain what I see.

A leaflet is no use
To define my feelings for you;
A magazine is no good
The pages are too few.

A diary won't do,
It only deals with each day,
A journal is not enough
To report everything you say.

A tabloid newspaper? No,
I have too many stories.
Even a broadsheet won't do,
To convey your glories.

A paperback is inadequate
There is not enough space;
A hardback won't do justice
To the words I want in place.

A reference book is almost right,
To describe your personality;
But it's an encyclopaedia I need
To praise you, in totality.

Don't Blame the Rain

Don't blame the rain,
Don't blame the clouds;
There's some chemical in your brain,
That's screaming out loud.

Don't blame your family,
Don't blame your past,
That's not the reason
You're getting nowhere fast.

Don't blame the weather,
Don't blame the atmosphere;
That's not the reason
Why you didn't get there.

Don't blame the food you ate,
Don't blame what you drank last night;
You got out the wrong side of the bed,
Now nothing's going to go right.

Don't blame fake news,
Don't blame the TV;
It's just up to you
To get where you want to be.

Don't blame the neighbours,
Don't blame the locality;
You're the same person in town
As you are by the sea.

Don't blame your education
Don't blame your schools;
If God's given you good health,
You have all the tools.

Don't blame the world situation,
Don't blame battles and wars;
If your life isn't going right,
Well, it's you that's the cause.

Don't Bombard Me

Don't bombard me with your questions,
Don't constantly hassle me,
Don't demand action now
Don't dare pressurise me.

I need to go for a walk
I need to get fresh air
I need to go outside
I need to see what's there

Don't make your judgement,
Don't be disappointed in me,
Don't come to conclusions
Don't categorise me.

I need to leave the room
I need to feel I'm free
I need to see what nature's doing
I need to just be me

Don't discuss my shortcomings,
Don't give me marks,
Don't consider my future
Don't put me on a chart.

I need to listen to birds
I need to look at the sky
I need to see grass and flowers
I need to be pacified.

Now you can listen
Now you might get some sense,
Now I'll seem quite normal,
Now there's no defence.

Drama in the Trees

There's high drama in the trees;
The birds are sounding frantic.
What is nature's trial,
Causing distress all the while?

A predator has arrived?
A fox at the tree base?
Or a cat, more scary,
Could reach their eyrie.

I want to help them,
But they don't need me.
God has given them wings;
No fox or cat has such things.

But I ask the little birds,
Can you help me, please,
Escape my predators
War, accidents, disease.

The little birds said to me
Yes we will help you,
Because you feel such love
For your friends who fly above.

Every time you feel pain,
We will make things right.
Our song will fill the air,
Listen, your mind will clear.

When there's drama in our trees
We can be like the birds
We may not have wings
But we can hear them sing.

Clarion notes fill the sky
There just for us,
Making the dramas of our day
Very soon fly away.

Chapter 5
Elysian Fields

Elysian Fields

The peacock shall be king,
The swan shall be queen,
The wise owls shall govern
Happiness shall reign supreme.

The eagles shall form the air force,
The foxes shall patrol the land;
The seagulls shall form the navy,
Guarding against contraband.

The water sprites guard the lakes,
The elves keep the trees,
The horses control the fields,
All creatures shall be free.

The sun shall rule the day,
The moon shall rule the night,
Morpheus shall guard our dreams,
Making sure they're all right.

There will be no schools,
But children will have their say,
Learning from mother nature
In every possible way.

All shall dine at banquets,
All shall drink nectar wine;
And dance the night away
Having a wonderful time.

We shall live forever,
There'll be no death or disease;
There'll be no depression or sadness,
We shall all be at ease.

So when the current government
Really doesn't appeal;
Imagine, take yourself away
To the beautiful Elysian Fields.

Chapter 6
Fallen Tree

Fallen Tree

The old tree blew down in the wind,
Shattered branches littering the path.
I'd walked past that tree for fifteen years,
Now it's something from my past.

Farewell my friend, lying there.
You'll be missed not just by me;
Because people, animals and birds
Got comfort from that tree.

Little birds rested in their nests,
High up amongst the leaves;
Squirrels hid nuts in its trunk,
Safe from marauding thieves.

People took shelter there,
Getting relief from the midday sun;
Loving couples stealing kisses;
Being spotted by no one.

The air was freshened by the tree,
Which removed the nasty gases;
Taking away the pollution
Which badly affected the masses.

The tree was connected by its roots
To the other trees around.
Now when they try to talk to it
There's no friend to be found.

This time man didn't kill our tree,
It was done for by the gales.
It tried so hard to withstand them,
But, alas, it failed.

Let's hope that the same winds
Collected up the tree's essence
And blew it to some other place
To create a beautiful presence.

So that something new can grow
From the poor forgotten stump,
To create a wonderful new tree
From which little squirrels can jump.

Finding you in the city

I walked through the streets
Of this city, this place
Searching art galleries
For pictures of your face.

I searched the libraries
In their literary glory
To find the books
That told your story.

I visited theatres
Watching all the plays
To see if they acted out
Your life in some way.

I went to cinemas
Hoping films I'd seen
Relived your life
On the silver screen.

I entered the Commons
The great chamber of debate
To discuss the life
Of my dearest soulmate.

I listened to voices
Of crowds in the street
Hoping to hear one say
With you they did meet.

I went into shops
In all the avenues
To see if they sold
Mementos of you.

I entered the markets
With all their nice stalls
You weren't there
So I visited the malls.

I went to the post office
And handed to the clerk
A note to you
With words from my heart.

But it was no good
I'd had enough of this.
I decided that to return
To my previous bliss

I'd head to the station
And take a train
Which led to your house
And never leave again.

Flower in the Forest

There's a flower in the forest,
A blossom on the tree,
A star in the sky
And a planet I can see.

There's a note in the music,
A rhythm in a song,
A lovely melody
I want to sing along.

There's a word in a sentence,
A chapter in a book,
A verse in a poem,
I have to take a look.

There's a scene in a ballet,
An act in a play,
Am image in a film,
So much more to say.

There's s colour in a painting,
A composition in a photo,
A scene in a video
Making me want to go.

These make happy moments,
They make life worthwhile;
When I think of them
I just want to smile.

Fluffy White Clouds

Fluffy white clouds are in the sky today,
A gentle breeze nudges them on their way.
The leaves on the rose bush nod in agreement,
But their branches and roots restrict their movement.

A little bird sings a sweet note,
Background music, to which the clouds float.
My patio door swings open and closed
In time with the clouds and the rose.

A blackbird flaps his wings to the rhythm,
Not haphazard, but with precision.
But the pigeons just sit together,
Just the same, whatever the weather.

As long as the clouds are fluffy, I'm fine,
But they're prone to gather in this country of mine,
And when they do my spirits fall,
But this is England, after all.

From good to bad, the weather changes;
Between opposite extremes, it ranges,
And if the clouds suggest my fate,
I think to myself, just wait!

Flying High

Flocks of birds, soaring so high
Loving their life, because they can fly.
Looking down at our pathetic lives,
Nations fighting, just to survive.

They glide gently, without a care,
Watching everything that goes on down here.
They know more than us, in their wisdom.
How I envy them, with their freedom.

Freedom from love, freedom from hate;
They surrender themselves to their fate,
To search for food all day long
It's right for them, nothing is wrong.

They watch us, and wonder why
We conjure up plots, plans and lies.
They never have need for any such thing.
They love their time on the wing.

Soaring through sunrise, daytime, sundown,
Then find a tree to settle down.
Covering little faces with their feathers,
Dreaming of fields flowers and heather.

Oh, little birds I envy you.
Tell me how to do what you do.
Teach me to live without a care,
Then maybe one day I'll join you there.

Forget the Bad Days

Forget the bad days
Forget what they say
Forget the bad vibes
Forget the cruel jibes.

Forget the bad news
Forget people's views
Forget the bad weather
Forget hate forever.

Look forward to eating good food
Look forward to being in a good mood
Look forward to seeing the sun
Look forward to meeting your loved one.

Look forward to hearing music
Look forward to feeling fantastic
Look forward to viewing good art
Look forward to taking part.

Some days there's no hope
And our spirits can't cope
Wait! Always remember this:
The next day will be bliss.

From my Kitchen Window

I look out of my kitchen window,
I see houses, trees and sky.
In each of the houses
Life is passing people by.

Behind the windows,
Within the walls;
In the bedrooms
Or in the halls.

People could be struggling,
With their minds and their health,
Whether they are in poverty
Or have great wealth.

But just beyond the house,
Are trees in all their glory,
In bright full leaf,
This is nature's story.

Behind the windows,
Underneath the roof,
Hidden behind curtains
You may find proof

Of joy and laughter
Where life is good.
You'd find happiness there
If search you would.

I look above, to the
Blue sky, with birds aloft;
We're all God's creatures
But sometimes… we get lost.

Chapter 7
Gilded Mirror

Gap in the Hedge

I saw a gap in a hedge
I wished I were a child,
Small enough to crawl through
Into a new world, wild.

Nobody would know I was there,
Except the local cat,
And a squirrel with whom
I could have a little chat.

I could hide from adults;
They'd never find me there,
With secret little objects
Which were in my lair.

And when people were nasty,
I could escape to my hideout.
I wouldn't care
If they scream or shout.

When I'm in my hideout
Nothing can trouble my mind,
I don't have to care
If people are horrible or kind.

I can watch the world go by;
Not take part, just observe,
Getting some peace
Which I rightly deserve.

And when it's quiet out there,
And the fracas has died down,
I'd creep out of my little den
Back into the busy town.

Life will be better,
I know I could cope,
Because when things got bad,
Off I would slope

To my gap in the hedge;
And I must confess:
There's no better place
To ease my stress.

Gilded Mirror

Looking into the gilded mirror,
It clouds over and I can see
The magic moments of a life gone by,
Tugging at the very heart of me.

A child running in the garden
With his puppy at his heel
A house full of family,
And the emotions they feel.

Then teenage years, with angst,
But I had my own little space.
My room, so sacred to me
For keeping away from the race.

Lives racing by,
All over far too soon;
But the house goes on,
Welcoming each new moon.

Childhood youth, middle-age,
People no longer here,
Hope, ambition reality,
Happiness, anxiety, fear.

The mirror gazes back
Simply reflecting reality;
Above an empty shelf
Where ornaments should be.

There are no ornaments now
Only dust and dirt
The house is crying
It is truly hurt.

But soon there will be new owners
A new family, new life,
Filled with new furniture,
A baby, husband and wife.

But we have not gone away
Our spirit still runs deep;
We are still with you, our house.
Don't cry for us, don't weep.

Girl in the Painting

With a daub of paint
With a flick of the brush
With a bit of watercolour
I create her.

With a mark from a crayon
With a bit of oil pastel
With a stroke of the pencil
I enhance her.

With oil paints
With some acrylic
With some collage
I perfect her.

And when she is created
And looking down at me from the wall
And when I'm bored with her
I reject her.

And start afresh.
But she's always there
She never changes
But I grow older.

Chapter 8
Heron

Haunting Music

A note from the piano,
A mystical panpipe,
A flourish from a violin,
Inspires me to write.

A soprano voice,
A riff on a guitar,
A sound from a keyboard,
My imagination goes far.

A celestial choir,
A roll of the drums,
Drives me to create,
Whatever may come!

The paint flows from music,
It follows the haunting tune,
Which inspires my hand
To create something soon.

The orchestra plays
And my spirits soar;
Should I paint, or write?
I'm not really sure.

Heron

The heron stood in the lake,
Looking graceful and serene.
Standing, not moving
Watching something unseen.

I asked him what he thought,
When he was standing so still.
He said he was thinking
Of the old house on the hill

Thinking of the days
When this estate was not here.
When airmen and women
Came down to the lake to share

Their private moments
Away from the horrors of war,
But they are not here now;
They are no more.

He told me of the days
When he was a chick in the nest,
And his parents taught him
What to do for the best.

They told him that
Although he was just a bird,
He was not ordinary…
Majestic is perhaps the word.

They told him that humans
Would be fascinated by his sight;
He would give them pleasure,
They'd dream of him by night.

I told him that was true
And he was my lakeside friend,
And although our lives are hard,
Our friendship would never end.

Hoping Things Get Better

We thought things were better,
But they started to get worse.
We must turn to music,
Art, and verse.

Music will inspire us,
And keep us in thrall,
So when news is bad
We won't mind at all.

Art refreshes our minds
And gives us hope,
And helps fix lives
Which we considered broke.

Poetry takes effort but
It's worth it in the end.
It stops us from falling,
And going round the bend.

God sends these things
To refresh and inspire
To rescue our souls
And lifts spirits higher.

House for Sale

House for sale,
Bricks and mortar,
But the memories it holds
Will never alter.

Long garden,
Not overlooked,
Where I played with my puppy;
He gave love, I took.

Nice bedrooms,
Some of good size,
Where I discovered adolescence,
With much surprise.

Cosy lounge,
With wooden beams.
Where my parents entertained,
But I was nowhere to be seen.

Here was the greenhouse
Behind it was my den,
Where I hid my secrets,
Which were so special then.

Here is the kitchen,
Scope for expansion,
Where my mother made meals
Fit for a mansion.

Here is our house,
Soon to be sold,
But what's not for sale
Is its part of my soul.

How will we be Remembered?

Will we be remembered
For our wonderful offspring,
And our children's children
And the joys that they bring?

Will we be remembered
For what we have created,
Works of art,
Forever feted?

Will we be remembered
For our written words,
In countless books
About which all have heard?

Will we be remembered
For the things we taught,
For the imparting of knowledge,
Which our pupils sought?

Will we be remembered
For the kindness we brought
To adults and children,
Always in their thoughts?

We will be remembered
For the things we do,
How we made people feel,
With their spirits renewed.

Chapter 9
I Feed the Birds

I Feed the Birds

I have bad thoughts
About people I don't like.
I've sworn in my car
At people on a bike.

But I feed the birds

I've lost my temper
When I should have been calm.
If people have annoyed me
I've wished them harm.

But I feed the birds

I've been aggressive
When I should have been kind.
When I'm wound up
I speak my mind.

But I feed the birds

My thoughts are not pure
And nor are my actions.
I've given to charities
But only fractions.

But I feed the birds

I've sworn at the TV
When it opposes my views.
I'm not competing
But I want people to lose.

But I feed the birds

I hate noisy neighbours
My patience is thin
The thoughts I have
Are probably a sin.

But I feed the birds

I'm not religious
I should pray more
Oh well,
It's not against the law.

So on reckoning day
When God recounts what He's heard,
He should remember

I fed the birds.

I Switch on the Light

I switch on the light,
But I wish it was the sun,
It's a poor substitute,
But it has to be done.

I open the window,
But I wish I was out in the breeze;
There's air coming in,
But I'm not at my ease.

I watch the television,
But I wish I was watching the sea;
With waves retreating,
And returning back to me.

I switch on the radio,
But I wish it was the sound of the birds
A far more soothing sound
Than what is heard.

I turn on the tap,
But I wish it was a river's sound;
Gushing and gurgling,
It's where water sprites abound.

I walk on my carpet,
But I wish it was grass;
With daisies and daffodils,
Redolent of my past.

I climb up the stairs,
But I wish I was climbing a hill;
Views from my landing window
Do not give me a thrill.

Nothing really compensates
For nature's delight.
Fear not! It'll return
At the end of the night.

If all the Minds in the World

If all the minds in all the world
Were used to create great things,
Can you imagine what we'd achieve,
Instead of aiming our thoughts within?

Instead of feeling depressed,
Our minds could be used to create
Thrilling works of fiction
Which cause much debate.

Instead of feeling down
Our hands could be used to create
Beautiful works of art
Depicting objects of every shape.

Instead of feeling low,
Our minds could be used to create
Tuneful melodic music
That everyone appreciates.

Instead of feeling sad,
Our minds could be used to create
Operatic works
Depicting a heroine's fate.

Instead of feeling negative,
Our minds could be used to create,
Enchanting movements of ballet,
Which, into our souls would penetrate.

Instead of feeling tearful,
Our hands could be used to create
Lovely objects of sculpture,
Taking such skill to make.

Instead of feeling defeated,
Our minds could be used to create,
Intriguing scientific inventions,
Using maths to calculate.

If all the minds in the world
Were used to create great things,
This world would be a better place,
For us and our offspring.

If I Seem Distant

If I seem distant,
My mind is up with the birds,
Soaring skywards,
Not hearing a word.

If I seem far away,
I'm imagining I'm a swan,
Floating gracefully,
Bothered by no one.

If I seem glazed-over,
I'm thinking about a bee,
Feasting on flowers' beauty,
Smoothly, effortlessly.

If I seem vague,
I'm a magician in a fantasy,
I wave my magic wand,
And I'm where I want to be.

If I seem not all there,
I'm on my special place,
Hearing ethereal music
With that look upon my face.

If I ask you to repeat,
Don't take offence
You'll eventually get me back,
You'll eventually see some sense.

Imagination

The heavier the rain
The greater my imagination
The more beautiful are the beaches
That appear inside my mind.

The stronger the wind
The greater my imagination
The bluer is the sky
That appears inside my mind.

The colder the air
The greater my imagination
The warmer the sand
That appears inside my mind.

The thicker the ice
The greater my imagination
The greener is the grass
That appears inside my mind.

The denser the fog
The greater my imagination
The more sparkling is the sea
That appears inside my mind.

The deeper the snow
The greater my imagination
The brighter are the flowers
That appear inside my mind.

But I don't mind
When nature isn't kind
Because I always find
That I'm not confined
I leave reality behind.

In Defence of the Realm

Will you defend my realm?
Will you provide my guard?
Will you watch my back?
Will you protect my yard?

Will you erect a barrier?
Will you put up a fence?
Will you reason with my foes?
Will you make them see sense?

Will you thwart their path?
Will you place a decoy?
Will you put them off?
Will you have a ploy?

Will you keep them distant?
Will you protect my space?
Will you give me warning?
Will you stop their race?

Will you argue my case?
Will you give me support?
Will you impart wisdom?
Will you explain my thoughts?

You will do this, I know,
You will not desert me;
You will always be my partner
You will be mine, to eternity.

In the Garden

In every blade of grass,
In every leaf on the tree;
In every branch from a trunk,
Nature is there to see.

In every twig from the branch,
In every coloured berry;
In every weed that grows,
There is reason to be merry.

In every bit of moss,
In every pretty flower;
In every small plant,
I see nature's power.

In every bit of soil,
In every crawling worm;
In every small pebble,
life is to be affirmed.

In every fluffy cloud,
In every bit of sky;
In every bird that passes,
I find the reason why.

In every sunlit place,
In every bit of shadow;
In every dappled spot,
Nature's got such a lot.

Sitting in my garden,
Is really the place for me;
It beats sitting in an armchair
That's not the place to be.

Is there a God to whom you pray?

Is there a God to whom you pray
Each and every day?
To whom you confide
Things which you normally hide?

Your God may be in the sky
Way above where the birds fly;
Your God may be down below
Where the winds blow and the water flows.

Your God may be in the voice
Of the newborn, it's your choice;
Or the eventual peace
Which falls upon the deceased.

Your God may be in musical notes
Through the air they float;
Or maybe special words that are said,
Or the best that you've ever read.

Your God may be in the petals
Of flowers on which bees settle;
Or maybe in the trees,
Leaves swaying in the breeze.

Your God may be in prayers,
To keep you from your fears;
Or maybe in wondrous icons,
Which you may shower gifts on.

Your God may be a He or a She,
Or whatever it is you want to see;
Whatever puts your mind at rest,
So in your God's eyes you are blessed.

A God is sometimes all you need,
Upon which your emotions feed;
There is no doubt in my mind,
Seek a God, and thou shalt find.

Chapter 10
Just Another Day

Job Satisfaction

I got no job satisfaction, but
The birds were singing.
It was a great success.

I was ignored, but
The sun was shining.
It was a great success.

My poems didn't come, but
The sky was blue.
It was a great success.

My paintings didn't work, but
The flowers were bright.
It was a great success.

Nobody could understand me, but
The air was fresh.
It was a great success.

I had a bad day, but
The stars were bright.
It was a great success.

There was nothing on TV, but
I saw a shooting star.
It was a great success.

The news was dire, but
There was a pleasant breeze.
It was a great success.

I was depressed, but
You were sweet.
It was a great success.

I couldn't sleep, but
The moon was full.
It was a great success.

Whatever happens
There's always something good.
It's a great success.

Just Another Day

I get up, out of bed,
Analysing what's in my head,
From the bed sheets, where I lay,
Just another day.

I put on the radio, to hear,
Whatever's happening out there.
It doesn't matter what they say,
Just another day.

I look out, up at the sky,
Asking the birds flying by:
Should I go out, or stay,
Just another day.

I may feel happy or sad,
Sometimes the thoughts are bad,
It's always been that way,
Just another day.

I'd like to go to the coast,
It's what I'd like the most;
Not allowed to see the bay,
Just another day.

When it's cloudy and dull,
I get pensive, and mull;
Longing for the sun's rays,
Just another day.

I hope things will change soon
And be a brighter afternoon,
Otherwise, it's mental decay
Just another day.

Chapter 11
London by Night

Lamppost Number Twenty-two

If you want to meet,
Come to lamppost number twenty-two.
Then we'll decide what we're going to do.

It's on the promenade, by the sea,
Is lamppost number twenty-two.
I actually think it's quite new.

Electrical current surges
Up lamppost number twenty-two
Giving light of a strange hue.

If you want to dead-drop secrets,
Use lamppost number twenty-two.
It's known to the privileged few.

If you want dodgy dealings
Meet at lamppost number twenty-two.
Legal or not, it's up to you.

During the day, it looks good,
Does lamppost number twenty-two.
By night it's a different view.

Some of the things that have happened
Under lamppost number twenty-two,
Would turn the air blue.

Sometimes boats land
Near lamppost number twenty-two.
You'd better not speak to the crew.

Whispers in dark corners
Mention lamppost number twenty-two;
Many mysteries to accrue.

Your reputation will decline,
Associated with lamppost number twenty-two.
You may have to sue.

I've heard of international intrigue
Connected with lamppost number twenty-two;
These things are best eschewed.

As lampposts go
I recommend lamppost number twenty-two,
And I've passed quite a few.

London By Night

Watching London by night
I stood at the top of the hill.
Watching the pretty lights
Gave me quite a thrill.

I decided I needed
To follow the enticing glow,
So I set out on my journey,
Which I'll describe below.

First I sought the white lights.
I found a small street.
But somebody told me about the knife crime
And said, "Be careful who you meet."

So I sought out the red lights,
Amongst buildings modern and tall.
But a terrorist had attacked
And I saw somebody fall.

I saw some yellow lights,
It looked a very nice place.
But there was threat of a pandemic
So it was now an empty space.

I found a green light;
It was making the traffic flow,
But with all that pollution,
I just had to go.

I'd had enough of all this.
There was no more to be seen.
I went back to my hill
The best place I'd been.

The grass is greener on the other side;
Even by night.
Try it for yourself,
And you'll see that I'm right.

Lonely Path

The lonely path beckoned me
To where I didn't want to go.
For some strange reason I ventured
To a destiny I did not know.

By the time I had doubts,
The trees closed up behind me.
I wished you were here,
Then maybe we could get free.

But there was only me.
I was totally alone,
And there was no signal
On my mobile phone.

Branches formed strange shapes;
There were stubs of trees,
Shaped like weapons,
All pointing at me.

The wind picked up,
The leaves started to shake.
I felt a pain in my head
And my legs began to ache.

Up ahead was a house,
The windows covered in ivy.
Creepers hid the door,
I felt someone behind me.

But there was nobody there;
Only the ghosts,
And when I knocked on the door
Rats scuttled from their posts.

The moon was coming up,
The bats squeaked all around.
An owl hooting
Was the only other sound.

What mysteries were held
On the other side of the door?
I didn't wait to find out,
I could stand no more.

Many years later
I passed that place.
It had been razed to the ground,
There was just an empty space.

But as I passed
I heard a whisper in my ear.
It said, "Don't forget us.
We are still here."

Look Up at the Sky

I go out to look at the sky,
Every night before bed;
I look at what's happening,
And it works wonders in my head.

Venus, Mars, the moon,
The Plough, Orion's Belt;
They're all there, I'm not alone,
And that feeling is heartfelt.

We can't get to all of them,
But they influence us so much;
In literature, in music, in love,
So many aspects are touched.

The crescent moon, at month's start,
Fills us with anticipation.
The full moon is a spotlight
Did we meet our expectations?

Venus, the Evening Star
Symbol of eternal love;
If things are not right with him or her,
We can get comfort from up above.

Sirius, the Dog Star
Flashing messages so bright;
Telling us what to do,
Making sure we get it right.

And above it all, the Milky Way
So distant, but who knows?
Maybe God resides there,
And, sometimes, He shows.

Lost on the Mountain

Sometimes at the foot of the mountain,
When the mist swirls over the peak;
When the darkness begins to descend,
I think I can hear them speak.

Two souls were lost
One sunny autumn day,
When the mountain played its tricks,
And made them lose their way.

When the gentle breeze blows
Their laughter fills the sky,
But when the gale starts
I realise it is their cry.

Oh, mysterious mountain
Sombre daunting presence;
Tell me what happened
I can still feel their essence.

Bring them back home
When the spring comes around;
I want to know they're safe,
And at last they can be found.

But the mountain won't speak to me;
It is wrapped in its misty veil,
And I creep away disappointed,
With no end to this sorry tale.

Chapter 12
Magic Horse

Magic Horse

There is a street nearby
Which leads to a farm.
I go there whenever
I need some calm.

There is a magic horse,
He and I have a link;
I tell him my thoughts,
He understands what I think.

When I can't solve a problem
I discuss it with my horse friend,
He thinks about it overnight
and solves the problem in the end.

I come back next morning
And look into his eyes
And the solution to my problem
Suddenly crystallizes.

Together we solve
The mysteries that I seek,
It doesn't really matter
If he really cannot speak.

The horse and I,
We can solve anything;
Whatever happens,
Whatever life brings.

Our equine friends
Are not just to ride;
I highly recommend that
In them you confide.

Magician

The magician stretched out his arm,
And the night turned to day;
The birds began to sing
In a wondrous way.

The magician raised his wand,
And the sun came out
And the clouds disappeared
And joy was spread about.

The magician uttered his spell,
And the sky turned blue
And the temperature rose
And we knew what to do.

I said to the magician,
"Can you make me a rich man?
Can you give me many things,
Be generous if you can."

He said, "I can give you riches
As much as you desire,
All the riches
You could hope to acquire.

"I can give you good health
Every single day.
I can give you kindness
You will not have to pay.

"I can give you creativity
To produce lovely art
And to write poetic words
That come from the heart.

"I can give you love
If you spread it around
So that, from others,
The love will rebound."

When things are not good
I can be heard to cry,
"Magician, oh magician!
Where are you?" I sigh.

But when I'm happy
And life is going well
I know my magician
Has cast his magic spell.

Major Route

My mind contains a major route
And some minor roads.
Direction of travel
Matters loads

Because when things are bad
I'm looking within my mind
The wrong direction of travel
I think you'll find.

I need to look outside of myself.
So set inward lights to red
And outwards lights
Are set to green instead.

Talking to people
Observing things
And all the good stuff
Which that brings.

Traffic must flow outwards
On the arterial route
When spirits are low
There's no dispute.

Some B roads can be open
Bringing traffic in
To top up my memory banks
That reside within.

But when all is good
All lights can be set to green
And I just hope
No collision is seen.

Message in a Bottle

I want to send
A message in a bottle,
Cast out to sea
Into the elements, free.

I'll not use Facebook
Or any social media;
I don't want to send to all,
I don't want anyone to call.

I don't care how long
It takes to be read
Instant gratification
Is not my vocation.

I don't care
What the fish think,
Or the whales;
I just want it to sail

To some distant shore
In an unknown location;
I just want to impart
A message from the heart.

I might put in the note
A return address,
So they can reply
Without using Wi-Fi.

They can cast it back
Into the waves,
And as the wind blows
It might just flow

Back to my shore.
Then I'll know:
Not Facebook friends
In the end,

Somebody cares enough
To send a message,
However long it takes
Which is not fake.

Missing the Sea

Wait for me, vast sea.
Wait for me, pebbles on the shore.
Don't forget me, seagulls,
I'll return, for sure.

Keep sailing, little sailboats,
Even though I'm not there to see;
Pretty colours on the horizon,
Providing stimulation for me.

Stretch out, long pier,
Although I'm not striding your length.
When the cruel sea lashes out,
Just maintain your strength.

I see you, Hengistbury Head,
Even though, just in my mind's eye,
Reaching out into the waters,
Proud cliffs standing high.

I'll soon be back, promenade
Pacing your seven miles;
But, just for now,
I think of you with smiles.

Misty Lake

Mist was swirling over the lake
Obscuring everything we know.
It's not just water vapour
There are spirits there; they don't show.

I asked the swan what was happening;
He seemed reluctant to reveal
The secrets of the lake
Which he would normally conceal.

He said sometimes God has to draw
A curtain over His creations,
So He can make adjustments
To improve our sensations.

He adjusts the sky to make sunshine,
He adjusts the clouds so they part,
He fiddles with the rain to make a rainbow,
So that it looks like a piece of art.

He does something to the water,
So the wind makes water sprites,
He carefully changes the temperature,
To make sure it's just right.

He makes the clouds look fluffy,
But ensures the sun shines through,
And if the weather gets out of control
He knows just what to do.

He doesn't like us to see all this,
So He makes the mist come down;
So that the mysteries of nature are hidden,
In countryside and town.

So said the wise swan,
Now you know the reason;
For this mystical swirling mist
in this strange magical season.

Moon

The moon and didn't warn me
That you'd steal my heart;
The stars didn't predict
That we would never part.

The universe was silent,
It didn't tell me why
My life would change
When you came by

The planets didn't envisage
Your effect on my mind;
Or the eventual peace
That I would find.

The galaxy was quiet;
It didn't foretell
The sound of your laughter
Like tinkling bells.

The shooting stars
Didn't catch my eye.
If they had done,
I would have realised why,

But I wasn't sure.
So on a clear cold night
I looked up above
At a star so bright.

Venus, goddess of love
Sent rays down to me,
So that I would realise,
I would see

That what you had
Was what I need.
Choose her, she said
And you will succeed.

Mother's Love

In all sorts of weather,
As soon as it gets light,
You'll find her in the garden,
And her eyes are so bright.

As she tends to her flowers
And encourages things to grow,
Just like the child she wanted,
But had to forgo.

She still has a mother's love
Somewhere deep inside.
When she's in her garden
It does not have to hide.

See the petals shine
In the early morning sun.
Look at the beautiful colours
So pleasing to everyone.

Then you will know that this woman
Has had a fulfilling life,
And all this was possible
Without being a wife.

My Abstract Painting

Come, see what I've produced.
It's an abstract painting; that you've deduced.
But if what you see doesn't seem real,
I've got news for you – it's what I feel.

A mass of blue, a splodge of white,
That's not abstract, it's the sky, all right?
An orange line, a yellow square,
That's a fruit bowl, oranges and lemons are there.

A purple area, with yellow and green;
That's bluebells and daffodils I've seen.
Brown marks, with some blue and grey;
Winter trees, with no leaves, I'd say.

Multicoloured spirals, what are they?
Oh, that's abstract, it was a difficult day.
Black strokes, grey hatching
Night drawing in, that's what I'm catching.

What's that blue line, with white?
The seaside, with waves catching the light.
Pink letters written in ink?
There's a message there, I think.

You may see an abstract mess,
It's more than that, I'd suggest.
The marks are generated by what's in my head
Showing the places I want to be, instead.

My Education

They taught me to add up,
They taught me to multiply.
They said two and two was four,
But I discovered that's a lie.

They taught me about battles,
They taught me all the dates.
They listed the kings and queens,
But they left me to my fate.

They taught me about chemicals,
They taught me about test tubes.
They explained about reactions,
But I had to take refuge.

They taught me about distant lands,
They taught me about cities.
They said the world is all different,
But I thought what a pity.

They taught me about friction,
They taught me about weight.
They said physics is important,
But they didn't tell me about hate.

They taught me religious education,
They taught me about the Bible.
They said I should believe in God,
But I discovered slander and libel.

They taught me all of the languages,
They taught me Latin and Greek.
They said it would help me progress,
But it just made me meek.

Forget all your teachings,
Forget all your schoolwork.
It's life experience that matters,
That you cannot shirk.

My Friend, the Little Bird

She sleeps in a nest
Lined with petals of rose,
On a mattress of feathers
In the hedgerow.

She awakes early
To dancing sunbeams,
Fresh from her sleep
And the sweetest of dreams.

She has her breakfast
Of dandelion pie,
And quenches her thirst
From the stream nearby.

She sings a sweet note
So humans can hear,
Which helps when their life
Seems too much to bear.

She knows what to do
During the day.
But her true purpose?
Who can say?

She knows that a cat
For her represents fear,
But to humans like me
She is something dear.

Dear little bird
Soar high in the sky,
And when you're tired,
Come back to lie

In your comfortable nest,
Where you make your bed,
Amongst the fragrant petals,
You lay your head.

My Ornaments

The glass duck gazes plaintively,
Out of my bathroom window,
Dreaming of Lake Garda,
And places he used to know.

The multicoloured parrot
Sits on my windowsill,
But he's thinking of Brighton
And wishes he was there still.

The brass heron
Watches from my bookshelf,
Remembering the charity shop
The home of his former self.

The painted cats
Live in my front room,
Where thoughts of Canterbury
Constantly loom.

The spindly giraffes
Either side of my hearth
Remember Bournemouth
Many years have passed.

The china elephants
Displayed behind my chair
Want to roam back
To Hampstead Antiques Fair.

The metal fish
From Salzburg's tourist street
Remembers fondly
The people he could meet.

Maybe that's where they go
At night when I'm asleep,
But when I'm looking at them,
All those memories I keep.

My Purpose in the World

The ant scurries around
Within the gaps in the crazy paving.
It has a job to do
With no time for personal craving.

The bee buzzes around
In and out of the flower,
Its purpose in life is to pollinate
And to give the queen bee her power.

The birds sing happily
Within the green-leafed trees;
They are there to sing
To make humans so pleased.

The dogs and cats are there
To give people such joy.
With dogs it comes naturally,
With cats it's all a ploy.

We humans are here
To meet and procreate,
To produce more human beings
That is our only fate.

But I have not done so
Is there a reason why I'm here?
If my poems touch one soul
Then my purpose is made clear.

My Yucca Plant

I love my yucca plant.
Don't ask me to get rid of it – I can't.
It's been with me through thick and thin,
Whether I lose or whether I win.

It was with me in my previous home
I brought it with me, and the garden gnome.
One of those things you just can't chuck.
It stays with me and brings me luck.

I give it a drink every few days.
It doesn't have demanding ways.
I hate to see its leaves wither.
If they do it makes a me shiver.

My yucca and I, we're a team,
There's more to us than it would seem.
If you come to my house for a cuppa,
Make sure you say 'h'´ to my yucca.

Mystical Music

The sunlight makes patches
Lighting the path, my road
With all different shapes.
Surely, it's a code.

I cannot go off the path
Because of the stinging nettles;
But up ahead I'm rewarded
With a patch of rose petals.

The wildflowers flash their colours
To somebody watching somewhere,
And the bees bring their nectar
To make honey we can share.

The trees talk, through the roots
To their neighbours, and further out.
I can't hear it but, to them,
It's loud, like a shout.

Deer whimper to each other,
The cows give meaningful looks.
The horses stand silent, but have
The wisdom of many books.

There's a flight path for insects,
And one for dragonflies.
The ragwort flashes yellow
And makes me empathise

With flora and fauna,
And the signals they emit
Such as a tree trunk that's dark,
And the other brightly lit.

The tree trunks entwine,
There's meaning in the shapes.
You need to take a reading
Using mystical measuring tape.

There's a trickle from the stream
Making me feel calm,
Like a religious feeling
Got from reading a psalm.

These signals have been flowing
Since the beginning of time,
When there was nobody to see them,
No one to make them rhyme.

But I'm here now,
So I'll give it a go.
When you're ready to understand,
You can visit my show.

Chapter 13
Nymph of the Winds

Night Sky

I go out into the garden,
I see the planets and moon.
Twinkling stars send me the word
That I must do something very soon.

Tell the people it's all right,
Tell them it'll be OK.
Stop the wars, don't fight,
There's always another way.

Tell them whatever they do,
We'll still be here,
Shining down on Mother Earth;
Somebody up here cares.

You can call it religion,
Or you can call it love.
Whatever it is that's there
There's something up above.

Watching over us,
Making sure we come through.
There is never an end,
Just something fresh and new.

Nymph of the Winds

You can see her on the lake
You can see her in the trees;
Hear the sound she makes,
And then you will believe.

She is the water sprite,
The nymph of the wind.
Try as you might,
You cannot rescind.

The effect of her power
Sometimes gentle, sometimes strong.
Watch the effect on the flower,
Nothing can be wrong.

The petals gently sway
To her persistent melody;
As if the flower says
Never leave me.

See her rustle
The still water of the pond,
Hear the gentle bustle
As the pond life responds.

Listen to her from beneath
The tall stately trees,
Moving from leaf to leaf
Exactly as she pleases.

Beware this nymph of the air
Maybe one day a breeze,
But you must always fear
And don't think she teases.

Because she can call her brother
The god of the gales.
He is quite another
Destruction will prevail.

Chapter 14
Out of the Houses

Oak Tree

I'm underneath the oak tree,
Fluffy clouds running free.
Strange bird nearby,
Hearing nature's sighs.

And I sigh too.
What can we do?
We are troubled, for sure
Everyone, rich, poor.

Green grass, white flowers,
A magpie approaches, with his powers.
I know the saying,
But I'm not playing

The game we're supposed to play
When a magpie stays.
Instead I think about me;
Not a good idea, says the tree.

The oak is right.
He has wisdom, and might.
He says, look at my leaves,
And the perfect symmetry I weave.

Look at the myriad flowers
Which nature has in her powers
To sprinkle amongst the grass.
Is it perfect, you may ask.

Children's voices, kicking balls
Thankfully they don't know all.
But beauty will show its face
When they join the race.

I see artists, I hear poets
I feel it, I know it.
These moments, remembered
For them, so tender.

I wish them friendship, and love
That will come from above.
They will achieve great deeds,
It's what we need.

Yes, said the oak, you're right
God will show them the light.
Don't you worry, all will be well.
Trust me, I can tell.

One Day we Shine

One day we shine
Like the dandelion.
And the next day we wilt.

One day we flow
Like the river goes.
And the next day we silt up.

One day we're bright
Like a floodlight.
And the next day we're switched off.

One day we sing
Like a bird on the wing.
And the next day we're silent.

One day we're strong
Like King Kong.
And the next day we're weak.

One day we ride around
Like a merry-go-round.
And the next day we're still.

One day we're delighted
Like a child who's excited.
And the next day we're flat.

One day our spirits are high
The next day we want to sigh.
That's the way it is.

One o'clock, Struck the Bell

One o'clock, struck the bell,
In the monastery in the woods.
The monks said their prayers
Faces hidden by their hoods.

Three o'clock, struck the bell,
In the priory's clock tower.
The children got excited,
Home in half an hour.

Five o'clock, struck the bell,
In the cathedral's tall spire.
The office girls got changed
Into their evening attire.

Seven o'clock, struck the bell,
In the church's tall steeple.
It was dinner time
For many hungry people.

Nine o'clock, struck the bell
In the castle's ramparts.
The birds were chattering,
So much to say before dark

Eleven o'clock, struck the bell
In the town hall's facade,
Some people were ready for bed,
Whilst others partied hard.

One o'clock, struck the bell
In the Gothic house in its grounds.
Nobody noticed the fairies dance
There wasn't a soul around.

Out of the Houses

Out of the houses
Into the fields,
Down to the beach,
Anywhere within reach.

See them flee
Into the air,
When the sun shines
The people find

Any other place
Where they can breathe
Away from the fumes,
Inhaling the perfume

Of the freshly cut grass
Or the stacks of hay
Or the salty sea breeze
Walking with ease.

Down by the river
Watching boats go by,
Seeing swans, serene
Like king and queen.

Down to the canal,
Along the towpath,
Seeing majestic houseboats
Proudly afloat.

They flee to the parks
With ornamental ponds,
Where children can run
Having plenty of fun.

Or into the grounds
Of castles so grand,
Seeing baroque parterres
Laid out with care.

Anywhere is OK
But not indoors,
And when the sun shines,
It'll all be fine.

Over My Fence and Far Away

Over my fence and far away
Are fields of corn and stacks of hay,
And far-off cities, full of folk
Who, like me, have fears and hopes.

They may speak different words
And hear the song of different birds,
But they are humans, as am I
Who are born, live and eventually die.

And now we suffer the same plague,
Let's be exact, and not be vague.
We cannot escape by travelling far;
We are the same, we are what we are.

I suppose you could be like Branson,
And buy an island for a king's ransom.
But you cannot escape your devils
As you tread the shore's pebbles.

So we may as well stay with others.
We are all sisters and brothers,
And it is our fate
To share common traits.

Leaders , followers, workers;
Academics, the talented, and shirkers.
Poets, artists, musicians,
Councillors, carers, physicians.

We just need to find our slot
And fill it with what we've got.
Be content with the cards we were dealt,
And eventually happiness will be felt.

Chapter 15
Poor little Buttercup

Pandemic Walk

Hundreds of trees
Bare branches pointing.
Mud everywhere,
Seeping, anointing.

Sunshine, some cloud
Promising, taking away.
Birds calling, some shrieking.
What are they trying to say?

People passing, no masks,
Dangerous even in fresh air.
The trees won't hurt me;
Good, because they're everywhere.

I cross a cattle grid,
Trying not to get stuck.
But OK, no problem
Cattle wouldn't have such luck.

Thoughts come and go,
Ideas take shape.
They just need to be stuck together
With some ethereal sticking tape.

I walk alone, it's best
Not even with my bubble.
She couldn't take the pace,
And then there'd be trouble.

This afternoon walk
To me it's obligatory.
My life without it
Wouldn't be satisfactory.

Parakeet

I wander through the street
In what seems tropical heat
Hearing the sounds of the parakeet.

It could be some sun-blessed isle,
But I'm walking single file
Socially distancing all the while.

In my dreams, I'd sigh,
God gives me wings and I fly
After wishing everyone goodbye.

Take me, parakeet, to where you belong,
Where you call out your shrill song,
Then all will be right, nothing wrong.

Away from pollution, away from fumes,
We'll smell the flowers' lovely perfume,
With so much space, so much room.

Just you and I, little parakeet,
In paradise we will meet,
With heavenly bliss at our feet.

Pollarded Tree

Tree, pollarded, cropped,
All its leaves have gone.
No more hiding places
For the squirrel to sit upon.

Just jagged, pointing branches,
Tree rings exposed.
It can't keep its age secret,
Because I can count those.

So much lighter in my flat,
So much more sunshine;
I'm so sorry squirrel,
If it's helped your decline.

I know your secret places
Are now exposed to all,
And there's nobody you can talk to,
Nobody you can call.

You'll find another tree
Which has its full complement
Of leaves, branches, acorns,
That will be a supplement.

And when you sit on the branch,
And give me a little squint,
Tell me what you're thinking,
Give me a hint.

Little Squirrel Nutkin,
Charming us all.
Are you preparing for autumn,
Which some call fall?

There's more room for you now
To swish your bushy tail,
As you leap from branch to branch,
Like a bird, you'll sail!

Poor Little Buttercup

Poor little buttercup,
One of many, a profusion.
People can trample on you,
Due to confusion.

Poor little buttercup,
You could make a good repast,
By a grazing cow
Who needs to eat, fast.

Poor little buttercup,
You're part of such a crowd,
The bee might ignore you
Although you're standing proud.

Beautiful little buttercup,
You're all I see.
Your radiant yellow glow
Gives such pleasure to me.

Pounding Pavements

Pounding pavements,
Or chasing them like Adele;
Walking over squelching mud,
Crossing grass as well.

Splashing through puddles,
Trying to avoid ice;
Trying to make the walking experience
Safe as well as nice.

Walking across roads,
Black tarmac, white lines;
Next to double yellows,
Where drivers get fines.

Crossing grass verges,
Avoiding evidence of dogs;
Sometimes in the woods,
Stepping over logs.

Do the thoughts in my head
Depend on the surface I'm treading?
Does the poetry conceived
Vary with the direction I'm heading?

I used to think academic thoughts,
But my efforts weren't needed.
Now I think poetic verse,
Which isn't totally unheeded.

A soft bit of grass,
I think of a good line;
A soft path,
I find a verse which rhymes.

The walk has distractions,
Some wanted, some not;
But I come back refreshed
I think, what a lot I've got.

Procession

The world was in a bad way;
In the future trouble lay,
So they formed a procession
With people from every profession.

There were people who were good
And did what they should,
And people who were bad,
And some who were mad.

They crossed mountains and hills
Passing barns and mills;
Joined by people in a tower,
Who once wielded power.

Now everyone was equal,
Waiting for the sequel
To their miserable life
In which problems were rife.

Up ahead was a light
That was burning bright,
But it was too far away,
So the people did say

Let us return,
Because our lesson is learned.
Let's start again
And end all the pain.

We'll take a sign
From He who is divine,
Let us advance,
And take the last chance.

Puff of Wind

A puff of wind blows
As I sit in the fresh air
And carries past me
without a care.

Why doesn't it stay
Why doesn't it hesitate
But goes on blowing
Through the garden gate.

Puff of air, so short-lived
I want to know
What becomes of you
When you leave me so.

I want to travel with you
To your next place
Whom do you affect?
In that other space.

Who else feels your touch
So soft on their face
Do you blow away their troubles
To some forgotten place?

Blow away the bad vibes
Bring in the good
You can improve somebody's day
I'm sure you could.

Pick up the beautiful thoughts
From everyone you brush
Take your time
No need to rush.

Then combine the beautiful things
Into a pot of wonder
Then wait for the bad days
When there's only thunder.

And visit all those afflicted
With their sadness
Brush against them
Take away their madness.

A thing of beauty
An oasis of calm
Making sure
They come to no harm.

Chapter 16
Regent's Park

Regent's Park

Some people walk
Some people talk
Roller boards rush by
Runners are on a high

Here in Regent's Park
With the cuckoo and the lark
There's sculpture and trees
Putting me at my ease

Nearby animals in the zoo
Want to take a look at you
Ducks busy in the lakes
They know what it takes

Terraces built by Nash
Needing millions of cash
A theatre amongst the roses
Actors faking poses

There was a college for girls
In their dresses and pearls
But now it's non-binary
So it's dull, no finery

In the lake, rowing boats
Where men who are woke
Let the girls take the oars
It's not against the laws

Not far away, pollution fumes
Overpowering the perfume
From the expensive stores
While the traffic roars

But here in Regent's Park
Uncontrolled dogs bark
I close my eyes, bliss
What I need is… this.

Rattler

The Rattler, they called it,
From a long-gone time;
Between the tall plane trees
Was this disused railway line.

Now I walk the path,
And hear the sound it made,
As it rattled on iron rails,
But with time, it fades;

Together with the lives
Of those who were onboard;
Long gone now,
They are with their God, their Lord.

But the trees are still there,
Though thicker in their girth,
Remembering the sounds of passengers'
Conversation, laughter, mirth.

There are houses nearby,
Where once there were only trees;
They hear not the sound of the train,
Only the birds and the bees.

But sometimes at dawn,
If you listen you can hear
The whistle of the guard,
As the signal says 'All Clear'.

Reasons to be Cheerful

A flower in the depth of winter,
A glimpse of dawn after a dark night.
A day of sunshine after the gloom,
An epiphany – I see the light.

A true note in a cacophony of sound,
A sweet fragrance after a stench.
A kind word after raised voices,
A dry spot after being drenched.

A soft touch after roughness,
Pretty colours after black and white.
A bird's sweet note after a storm,
I see a beautiful sight.

Parting clouds revealing a starry night,
The taste of food after being starved,
A strong drink after a bad day,
My troubles seeming halved.

God put all these things there for us
Because he needed to make us see,
That nothing is bad forever
And most of those things are free!

Red Kite

The red kite soars high
Over love over hate;
Hearts are being broken
But he just won't wait.

He has no time for that
King of the sky;
There are fields to fly over,
His prey will die.

Does the red kite know
What is in my heart?
When I see him soar,
And my emotions start

And I wonder,
Does he care, does he see
The effect he has
On you and me?

Soar, red kite, soar
Up into the heaven so high;
Is there anywhere
He can't fly?

He is on a mission,
See his strong wings;
There is land to cover,
Who knows what it will bring.

Red kite, red kite
Do you feel your power?
Does it please you
that lesser birds cower?

But I am not afraid;
You give me only hope,
Seeing you strong,
It makes me cope.

Because if God can create
Wonderful creatures like you,
He can give me the power
To see things through.

Rhythmic

Rhythmic, like the steam engine,
The moon going round the Earth,
The cycles of the seasons,
Death, followed by a birth.

Rhythmic, like my moods,
The beating of a bird's wings,
The revolutions of the planets,
Gloom, then joy the dawn brings.

Rhythmic, like falling rain,
The pigeon's raucous call,
The dolphin's leap from the water,
Heroic rise and fall.

Rhythmic, like the beating of a drum
The motors revolution,
The day, followed by the night
Muse's *Absolution*.

Rhythmic, like the beating of your heart
The steady breathing,
The ups and downs
Wounding, then healing.

Rhythmic, like the leaves in the wind
The day's work, then rest,
The week's work, then play
Which is worse, which best?

Rhythmic like the bassist's riff,
The dripping tap,
The dancer's movements,
On my door, postman's rap.

Rhythmic, like life itself
The good days, bad days
The ups and the downs,
The repeated turns through this maze.

Chapter 17
Silk Stream

She-Buddha

She sits in a yoga pose,
Like a Buddha, magnificent;
Legs folded beneath her,
Her aura is significant.

She absorbs the sun's rays,
And they fortify her soul;
She becomes rejuvenated,
After life takes its toll.

The sunshine produces her smile,
It gives her a big heart;
It fills her with goodness,
And we all receive a part.

The sunshine gives her kindness,
And makes her touch so soft;
And above her you might see
Angels flying aloft.

The sunshine affects her babies,
Which will surely be born,
It helps her love them,
Every eve and every morn.

Buddha girl, with your spirit
I want to be blessed;
And there will be enough
To share with all the rest.

Silk Stream

I go to the Silk Stream,
Glistening in the suburb,
Flowing like a dream;
Which I don't want to disturb.

Winding past houses
Washing away bad feelings
Between warring spouses
Bringing some healing.

Come with me to the stream,
Cast away your fears;
The reflection of the sunbeam,
Dries up your tears.

Throw in a little leaf,
And watch it float along;
As the babbling brook
Sings a little song.

Your troubles float away
Past the many water sprites;
There is a spell that they say
When the sunbeams are bright.

Making your troubles disappear,
And your mind become calm.
You will have no more fear,
And will not be alarmed.

The Silk Stream will soothe
All your stress away.
There's nothing to prove
It's just as I say.

In the Silk Stream you will have trust,
In the Silk Stream you will find peace,
There is no doubt, it must
Bring your release.

Sitting by the Lake

Sitting by the lake
Thinking about what you said,
Did you mean what I thought,
Or was it something else instead?

Should I get upset,
Should I be really sad?
Was what you said good
Or was it really bad?

I could ask the ducks,
But I don't think they'd really know.
The swans are no help either,
But they put on a really good show.

The water lilies are pretty;
They make a lovely sight.
But I don't notice, I just think
Should we get into a fight?

I tell my troubles by day
To all the waterfowl;
And if they won't listen, by night,
I tell them to the owl.

They all tell me, don't worry,
Just give it another day.
Then you'll be pleasantly surprised
By the things she will say.

So if you're in trouble,
And you're feeling really blue,
Go sit by the lake
Then you'll know what to do.

Sitting in the Garden

Sitting in the garden
Watching the sun go down,
The pigeon, blackbird and I
Just outside London town.

I, on my chair,
The blackbird on the fence
The pigeon on the blackberry bush
Everything made sense.

Each lost in our thoughts,
In completely different ways
With a different agenda
Towards the end of the day.

The blackbird called for his mate,
Listening for her call.
That was all that mattered to him,
Nothing else at all.

The pigeon ate his fill
From the bush full of blackberry
He takes his food where he can,
Wherever is the opportunity.

And I, what am I thinking?
What will the next day bring?
What will the future reveal?
Will it be to my liking?

But there we were
Three of God's creatures.
Two were similar,
But with different features.

Two birds and I,
Two out of three can fly,
But one day, we hope far off,
All will eventually die.

Sparkles

Where do all the sparkles go
On a cloudy miserable day?
Does nature put them in a box,
Or store them some other way?

Does God have a palette
And he uses just the grey?
If he'd ask me, use the blue,
Is what I'd truly say.

Where do all the sunbeams go
In dark and dismal weather?
Are they pushed back up to the sun,
Hopefully not forever.

They're stored up like a spring
Ready to be released
As soon as the clouds part
To make our happiness increase

Where do all our smiles go
When the rain comes down again?
It happens so often,
A regular refrain.

All we have to do
Is think of the sun
Then our spirits increase
Each of us, every one.

Spider's Web

Spider, spider, I am racked with guilt,
I destroyed the home you painstakingly built.
I was trying to make my home clean,
So there's now nothing where you had been.

At least I did not harm you,
You were free to see what you could do.
You crept off, not even a shirt on your back.
You had nothing, everything you lacked.

Yet here you were starting again
You had nothing to lose, everything to gain.
Crawling to the edge of the sill,
I have to admire your iron will.

I felt like Robert the Bruce,
Who watched the spider turned loose,
Try, try and try again,
It didn't think 'if', only 'when'.

You will climb again to the top
Your weaving skills will never stop;
Weaving again your intricate web
Your food source and your bed.

I'm so pleased my duster didn't destroy
Your little body, which you will employ,
To lure a fly, for your next meal,
And its destiny will be sealed.

And you'll keep on doing it until that time,
When God decides the very next line,
And you'll be simply dusted away,
And in the bin your little body will lay.

Spider, spider, you had no charm,
But I know you meant me no harm.
Keep on doing what you have to do,
I just know you'll see it through.

Spirits

My spirits are never sinking
When there's a star twinkling
And wind chimes tinkling
And leaves are crinkling
I've got no inkling
Of how my thoughts are linking
But are never sinking.

When a moonbeam's shining
My spirits are never declining
My stars are aligning
All this is defining
And I'm opining
That my mood is climbing
When a moonbeam's shining.

With a fresh breeze blowing
I'm always knowing
Seeds in my mind are sowing
And my face is glowing
I know where I'm going
My pleasure is showing
When there's a fresh breeze blowing.

When colours are so bright
On the flowers, after the night
I never have to fight
Because it's a delight
And a beautiful sight
In the bright daylight
God has done it right.

Strange Times

Things are not normal,
But the pigeon is in the eaves,
The daffodils are in bloom;
Soon there'll be green leaves.

There's birdsong in the garden,
The tulips are making a show;
But where it's all going to lead,
I really do not know.

I can see people from my window.
With some dogs in the park.
But it's better not to think too much
Because things are a bit stark.

We'll have to get used
To this new way of existence,
But to me what's important
Is nature's persistence.

Persistent in its beauty,
Persistent in its joy,
So we can all enjoy it,
Adults, girls and boys.

I heard a robin
And I saw a red kite
Soaring in the sky
Like a feather, so light.

I saw vapour trails
Of a plane high in the sky,
But where was it going?
Who's on board, and why?

There's no traffic to be heard,
But I can hear children playing,
And some adult voices, although
I can't hear what they're saying.

We can only thank God
That the day is warm and bright,
And see what He brings us
Hoping it's good and right.

Chapter 18
Twinkling Star

Take off your Headphones

Take off your headphones
As you walk underneath the trees;
Hear the music of the wind,
As it rustles through the leaves.

Take off your headphones
As you walk past the lake,
So you hear the magic sounds
Of the ducks and the drakes.

Take off your headphones
As you move under the canopy,
Hearing the woodpecker's sound,
Beating a rhythm for you and me.

Take off your headphones,
As you walk along the brook,
Hearing the little waterfall,
Over the stones, just look.

Take off your headphones,
So you can listen to the birds,
Creating the best music
That you've ever heard.

Take off your headphones
As you listen to life,
And for once just forget
About your troubles and strife.

The Ferryman

I went to the river's edge,
The ferryman was there.
I said, "Ferryman, ferryman,
Tell me your fare.

"How much do I pay
To escape from all this?
Take me to a place
Where there is happiness and bliss.

"I need a place
Where everyone is well,
Where life is good,
Not some sort of hell."

He said he could take me there
But the river is wide
And fraught with danger
Before getting to the other side.

But over there he'll show me
Just small ordinary things;
I'll appreciate them so much more
And feel like a king.

He said you won't take for granted
What you did before
And you won't be constantly
Searching for so much more.

On the other side of the river
There will be wondrous sights
Which you could not see before
But now it's all right.

On the other side of the river
Everyone will be kind
And if you're different from them
They won't really mind.

On the other side of the river
There will be less crime
Because of what happened
It will be a better time.

Come with me in my boat
And together we'll travel
To that better place
And your mind will unravel.

Life will be good
Life will be calm
My ferryboat and I
Will protect you from harm.

Tower

I'm building a tower.

All the lovely things you say
All the lovely things you do
All the funny words you use
All your funny expressions, too,
Make the first floor of my tower.

The wisdom that you have
The intelligence you show
Your perceptive mind
The things you know
Make the second floor of my tower.

All the beauty of your looks
All the personality that shines
All the friendliness in you
All the good things you find.
Make the third floor of my tower.

The tolerance you show
The tactfulness, so controlled
Your patience, and reserve
The stories you have told
Make the fourth floor of my tower

All the love you have for children
All the kindness in your soul
All the tenderness of your heart
All the things that make you whole
Make the fifth floor of my tower.

The clever things you say
The culture that you show
Your funny observations
The conversation that flows
Make the sixth floor of my tower.

I could go higher and higher
And build my tower up to heaven.
Another day; right now,
I'm stuck on floor seven.

Twinkling Star

My spirits are never sinking
When there's a star twinkling
And wind chimes tinkling
And leaves are crinkling
I've got no inkling
Of how my thoughts are linking
But are never sinking.

When a moonbeam's shining
My spirits are never declining
My stars are aligning
All this is defining
And I'm opining
That my mood is climbing
When a moonbeam's shining.

With a fresh breeze blowing
I'm always knowing
Seeds in my mind are sowing
And my face is glowing
I know where I'm going
My pleasure is showing
When there's a fresh breeze blowing.

When colours are so bright
On the flowers, after the night
I never have to fight
Because it's a delight
And a beautiful sight
In the bright daylight
God has done it right.

The Umbrella

Protect me from the bad day,
Stop the worry and stress.
It started off OK,
But good feelings got less and less.

I can hide under my brolly,
Pushing bad things away.
Pushing away the insults;
Not listening to what they say.

Chapter 19
Where is the Nightglow?

Walk

There's a road,
Cars drive past,
Houses either side.
I walk.

There's a lake,
Path alongside,
Ducks and swans.
And I walk.

There's a street,
Shops either side,
People about.
Still I walk.

There's a park,
People playing tennis,
Lots of dogs.
I must walk.

Why not run, they say?
Think about your body,
But I think about my mind.
So I walk.

Walk Through Nature

Over the branches
Up the bark
Hidden by the leaves
In the park
Through the grass
By the stream
Along the path
Water gleams
Amongst the shrubs
Between the weeds
On the ground
Grown by seeds
Across the lawn
By the river
In the forest
Old trees wither
On the water
In the lake
Seeing patterns
The ripples make
Crunching twigs
In the soil
Hanging catkins
Form a coil
Growing plants
Coloured petals

Green fern
Stinging nettles
Spreading foliage
Hanging fruit
Recent blooms
Fresh new shoots
Pretty flowers
Fresh bouquet
Giving pleasure
Is nature's way
Seeing God's beauty
All is fine
This is yours
And it's mine.

Waterfall

A giant waterfall
Fills the air with a roar
As the water comes rushing down
Swirling, searching for something more.

Then it becomes a river
Fast-flowing and wide.
Water still rushing
Past the reeds at the side.

Then it becomes a stream,
Gently falling over stones.
The sound is a trickle
Calming to our bones.

We start our lives with such force,
With energy and vigour,
Starting like a waterfall,
Then becoming a river.

Later life is like the stream,
Calmer than before.
Not making so much noise,
But never being sure

Which direction our flow will take;
It doesn't take much to obstruct.
But we hope the flow will continue,
And it will, with luck.

Waves on the Shore

Just like waves on the shore
You ebb and flow.
Something good comes in;
Something bad goes.

You bring in your love,
Take away my fear.
Bring in your peace
And leave it here.

You bring in your kindness,
Take away my hate.
Bring in your calm,
It compensates.

You bring in your humour,
Take away my bad mood.
Bring in your laughter
To me it's like food.

You bring in your smile,
Take away my frown.
Bring in your happiness,
Wear it like a crown.

You bring in your good nature,
Take away my low trust.
Bring in your confidence,
You say, I just must.

You bring in your friendliness,
Take away my hostility.
Bring in your heart,
With all your ability.

You bring in your sincerity,
Take away my lies.
Bring in your truth,
And stifle my cries.

Just like waves on the shore
You ebb and flow.
Something good comes in;
Something bad goes.

Weeping Willow

Weeping willow
For whom do you weep?
Your tears float away
Down the river at your feet.

Are you crying for humanity
Because of all of our mistakes?
You know the solution,
But your advice we don't take.

Are you crying for the environment
Which we are slowly polluting?
From the stores of nature,
Humans are looting.

Are you crying for the spirits
Of the long departed,
And the wisdom of the souls
That could have been imparted?

Weeping willow
please don't weep
because your magical beauty
you will always keep.

What Happened to the Birds?

What happened to the birds,
Friends that I once knew?
What has become of them?
I wish I had a clue.

What happened to the crow
Who I use to feed,
With my apple cores
That I would I no longer need?

What happened to the robin
Who got caught in my room?
If he's reading this,
Come back soon!

What happened to the magpie
Who I hope to see with his mate,
So that a lucky sighting
Can dictate my fate.

What happened to the pigeons
Who used to settle on my roof?
I had work done,
Now they're aloof.

What happened to the green woodpecker
Who laughed as he flew,
With an up-and-down motion
That he knew how to do.

What happened to the red kite
Who soared in the sky,
Who came from the Chilterns
To fly nearby?

What happened to the seagulls
Who came from the coast?
About their maritime stories
They'd always boast.

Maybe they are still with me
I just don't know,
Because they all look the same
Wherever I go.

But God doesn't mind
If I can't tell them apart,
Because always sends one
Straight to my heart.

What Happened to Your Dreams?

What happened to your dreams, where did they go?
Did they go to the end of the rainbow?
Were you ever told
About the pot of gold
Or were your dreams sold?

Did they go up to the clouds above?
Is that what happened to our love?
Did they go down to the sea?
Is that what happened to me?

Chase after your dreams
In sunlight they gleam
They're everything they seem
To you.

Before they escape
Don't ever wait
Before it's too late
For you.

What happened to your dreams, where did they go?
Did you drop them in the stream that flows?
Did anyone find them there?
Or did they blow into the air,
And with the birds were shared?

Did they melt in the sun
After they had begun?
So dear to your heart
Like such fine art.

Before they escape
Don't ever wait
Before it's too late
For you.

What Three Words?

What three words
Would I say to you,
When it's the same emotions we feel?

What three words
Would I say to you,
When we understand each other's heart?

What three words
Would I say to you,
When we share a lovely meal?

What three words
Would I say to you,
When we admire a work of art?

What three words
Would I say to you,
When you predict what I'll say?

What three words
Would I say to you,
When we've experienced the same past?

What three words
Would I say to you
When we think the same way?

"I love you."

When I can't Sleep

When I can't sleep
I let my mind wander free,
Into a clearing in the woods;
The full moon shines down on me.

From out of the trees steps a fairy;
Just like in a child's fable.
I can't quite believe my eyes,
But my mind ensures I'm able.

And this is what she says to me:

"Hold my hand and come hither;
Open your eyes to see.
Remember this when daylight comes,
Even though you'll forget me."

She took me to the river,
She took me to the sea,
She took me to the mountains
So much for me to see.

She took me to the streams,
She took me to the glades
She took me to the flowers,
To show what God has made.

She showed me waterfalls,
She showed me magic lakes,
She showed me lovely birds,
I heard the sounds they make.

She showed me the dark sky
She showed me the planets and stars,
She showed me the Milky Way
She showed me Venus and Mars.

She kissed me on the forehead
And soothed my troubled brow.
She closed my eyes and said,
"Go to sleep now."

And when the morning comes,
I think of my wonderful dream
Or was it the truth;
Where had I been?

When I hear Birdsong

When I hear birdsong,
If I could understand what they say,
Maybe my life would be easier,
In so many different ways.

When I touch the trees,
If I could feel their power,
Maybe I'd be happier
Every waking hour.

When I look at flowers,
If I could interact like bees,
Maybe I'd be nicer
To everyone I see.

When I smell the honeysuckle,
If I could remember that scent,
Maybe I would notice more
Things that are heaven-sent.

When I hear water trickling,
If I could remember that sound,
It would calm me so much
On any situation I found.

When I touch the petals,
If I could retain that feel,
Any emotional wounds
Would so quickly heal.

When I look at clouds,
If I could interpret their shape,
Maybe it would help me,
In the decisions I make.

When I hear, feel and see
Nature, by my side,
I know God is with me,
Here, far and wide.

When Normal Life Resumes

When normal life resumes
Do we go back to before,
With so many arguments
And so many wars?

When normal life resumes
Will the planet still be warming?
Can the environment be saved,
Have we heeded the warning?

When normal life resumes
Will the politicians agree?
Will they still be posturing,
Or will they help you and me?

When normal life resumes
Will the terrorists calm down,
And stop trying to destroy
Our cities and our towns?

When normal life resumes
Will neighbours get on better,
Or will every dispute end
In a solicitor's letter?

When normal life resumes
Will there be no more criminal acts,
With good deeds being done
Instead of violent attacks?

When normal life resumes
One thing of which we can be sure:
Nature's delights
Will be as good as before.

Where is the Night Glow?

Where is the night-time glow
From my beloved London town?
From my hill I could see it below;
Who's turned it down?

If I was to venture in
To those city streets so bare,
It would be a sin
To see no people there.

Traffic lights blinking bright
From red to amber to green,
But there are no cars in sight,
None to be seen.

Mannequins stare out
From once-lit shop facades,
It's like they want to shout:
Come in, use your credit card!

And from the once bright glass
Making all the office blocks,
Nobody works at their tasks,
And on the doors are locks.

The only bright light
Flashes from a police car
Warning anybody in sight:
Don't come this far!

But there's nobody about;
The city has lost its soul.
No hubbub, no shouts,
And it's taking its toll.

No terrorist could do this
To our wonderful lively town,
Now a plague's deadly kiss
Has brought it to the ground.

It's now a ghostly place;
But bring on the hour!
When the normal frantic pace
Returns to this city of ours.

Chapter 20
You are my Destination

You are my Destination

Show me a map to get to your heart,
Show me the map to your heart
I need to travel there before we part.
Which motorway do I take, or country lane?
I need to know, to see you again.

Do I take the high road or the low?
Will the map show me which way to go?
Where is the key to this map, so confusing?
I need to see it in case I'm losing.

Your love, kindness and affection;
Which map is it in the book, which section?
I want to go straight there, no roundabouts.
When I get to your place I won't go out.

Should I use a sat nav or a paper map?
I'll retry if I'm lost – I'm a persevering chap.
And if I come to some dead end,
It won't stop me, I'll find a bend

That I can speed round to be by your side;
I know very much it'll be worth the ride.
When I'm there the map will be thrown away,
Because I'll no longer go anywhere, I'll stay.

www.ingramcontent.com/pod-product-compliance
Lightning Source LLC
Chambersburg PA
CBHW040302170426
43194CB00021B/2866